Suits:
Happy cooking!
Christine Liu

營養食譜

The romanization used in this book is the "Pinyin" system from a dictionary:
Wang, Fred Fangyu: Mandarin Chinese Dictionary, Chinese-English. Seton Hall University Press, South Orange, New Jersey. Reprinted by Mei Ya Publications, INC. Taipei, Taiwan. 1972

About the Author

Born and raised in Shanghai, Mainland China, Mrs. Liu completed her college education at the National Taiwan University. It was there she met and married her husband, Stephen Liu, presently professor of Microbiology at Eastern Michigan University.

After the birth of their oldest son, the Lius lived awhile in the United States, then moved to Sao Paulo, Brazil where they remained for some years. The Chinese community of Sao Paulo was sizable and affluent and their cuisine was quite popular. It was during that time that Mrs. Liu kindled her latent interest in cooking which ultimately led to the writing of this book.

In 1965, the Lius returned to the United States and settled in the Ypsilanti-Ann Arbor area. Mrs. Liu further developed an interest in and took up the study of nutrition at the University of Michigan. She received her Masters degree in Nutrition in the School of Public Health in 1971. Later on she did further graduate studies in the department of Food Sciences and Nutrition at Massachusetts Institute of Technology.

For some years Christine Liu has contributed her cooking and teaching talent to the Ann Arbor community by teaching Creative Chinese Cooking and Nutrition & Diet at the Continuing Education Department of Ann Arbor Public Schools. This book represents the culmination of her years of cooking and teaching experiences and creative approach to Chinese cuisine. With a background in Chinese culture, combined with a thorough knowledge of nutrition, Christine Liu offers a unique and artful approach to the world of fine cooking and good eating with the added plus of a deep concern for good nutrition.

Book design and illustrations by Jacqueline Sharp

NUTRITION AND DIET WITH

CHINESE COOKING

BY CHRISTINE Y. C. LIU, M.P.H.

Graphique Publishing   Ann Arbor, Michigan   1985

ACKNOWLEDGMENT

I wish to acknowledge the invaluable assistance given to me by Jacqueline (Jay) Sharp. As a trained artist, Jay has done a wonderful work of illustration, and it has added a new dimension to my book. In addition, Jay has worked with me in designing, editing and many other aspects of the book. With her assistance, I am able to have this book published at the earliest possible date. As a result of our working together, both Jay and I have become good friends — an added blessing!

I also would like to express my thanks to the staff of the Continuing Education Department of the Ann Arbor Public Schools and to the staff of the University Extension Service. It has been my privilege to teach courses for the last several years in these departments. To many of my professors, friends and to the students who took the courses, I should say "thanks" for their encouragement, enthusiasm, and trust.

Above all, my special thanks to my dear husband, Stephen. From the beginning and to the completion, I have received all the necessary encouragement and cooperation from Stephen. His love and interest in the work have sustained me in the long hours of working on this book. To our children, Ted, Paul, Becky and Peter, I should say that you all have been very good to me while I spent hours writing and experimenting with the recipes in order to have them "perfected."

As always, I shall welcome comments and constructive criticism from readers and users of this book.

To:
Stephen, Ted, Paul, Becky and Peter

Table of Contents

1. Introduction 1
2. Is Chinese Food Nutritious? 4
    The protein facts
    Other advantages
3. About Monosodium Glutamate (MSG) 7
4. Custom, Chopsticks and Tea 10
5. Method of Preparation and Cooking 13
6. Cooking Utensils..................................... 15
7. Menu Planning 17
    Color, variety, timing, nutrition and diet,
    management and sample menus
8. Recipes
    A. Soup 24
    B. Meat 42
    C. Poultry.. 96
    D. Seafood 132
    E. Vegetables......................................164
    F. Bean Curd (To Fu) 192
    G. Rice, Noodles and Chinese Steamed Bread 220
    H. Eggs 242
    I. Desserts and Snacks (Dim-Sum)....................258
    J. Microwave Recipes...............................295
9. Chinese Ingredients and Seasonings................... 310
10. Tables and Charts
    A. Measurements and abbreviations 316
    B. Sources of important nutrients 316
    C. Desirable weight for selected heights............318
    D. Minimum daily requirements of calories,
        certain vitamins and minerals...................319
    E. Calories, protein, fat and carbohydrate
        value of foods used 319
11. Recipe Index 324
12. Menus Evaluated in Terms of Specific Nutrients........332
13. References 335
14. General Index......................................336
15. Order Blanks

Introduction

Among the world's great culinary arts, there can be little doubt that Chinese cuisine is one of the greatest and the most unique.

There are many elements that have influenced the development of this unique cooking style. First, the Chinese people are fond of eating. The joys of eating good food in China are greatly appreciated at all levels of society. Cooking has developed into a very sophisticated art. Confucius once said: "Eating is one of the basic natures of the human being." A delightful and delicious meal creates happiness, harmony, mental and physical well-being.

The second element that influenced Chinese cooking was the times of prosperity. In her long history of civilization, China and her people enjoyed "golden eras." When peace, good weather and intelligent leaders combined, both the people and the monarchs developed countless good recipes, philosophy of living and the finest of arts.

The third element is the scarcity of food. Because China has been an agricultural country for thousands of years, the Chinese people have always lived at the mercy of Mother Nature. During the lean years, people would explore everything edible to stay alive. Many strange and incredible ingredients such as wood ears, lily buds, etc. were discovered and added to Chinese recipes. The scarcity of food also taught people how to avoid waste. Various fruit and vegetable peels and even shark fins (after proper treatment) turned out to be delicacies in Chinese food.

Another important element is the dearth of fuel. Forest conservation, coal mining and oil drilling are relatively new. After thousands of years of consumption, very little fuel materials remained on the surface of the land. The need to save fuel became so influential that most Chinese dishes require a lengthy preparation but only a few minutes cooking time. With the current energy crisis the Chinese cooking method offers a practical way to conserve fuel while it delights the taste buds.

The fundamental principles of Chinese cookery are the same throughout China. The dishes must be colorful, the aroma must be appealing and the taste must be delicious. But because China is a vast country with poor transportation, diverse agricultural production and a varying climate, the people from each region began to develop their own specialties with their own distinctive spices.

Generally speaking, the people of the south-east region like light and sweet dishes. In the northern region, salty dishes are popular. In the south-west region, highly spiced and hot dishes are favored.

The variety of Chinese dishes seems almost endless. Since the turn of the century, especially during and after World War II, China has undergone a great change. More people have become urbanized. People from places all over China live together in urban communities. They exchange their cooking experiences and offer the distinctive dishes of their home towns. The younger generation of Chinese people has the privilege of learning all the good dishes and are seldom aware of where those dishes originated.

Most Chinese dishes are cooked with meat and vegetables together, so the foods contain lower calories and are less rich than Western style food. Vegetables stay bright and crisp by cooking them for a short time over high heat, either in their own juice or in a small amount of water. This method retains most of the vitamins and minerals. As a nutritionist, I am deeply convinced that the Chinese cooking method is the healthiest and that Chinese food should be considered as the diet of the future.

Since we eat not only for enjoyment but for good health, many people are very conscious of nutrition and diet. I have undertaken the task of compiling and evaluating the nutritional information for the recipes in this book. With this information you will know the number of calories, the grams of protein, carbohydrate and fat contained in the particular recipe. You will be able to make a "do-it yourself" diet with adequate amounts of important nutrients. The nutritional value of Chinese food and that of monosodium glutamate (MSG) are discussed in the sections "Is Chinese Food Nutritious?" and "About Monosodium Glutamate."

Almost all the recipes, except the very simple ones, have been repeatedly tried and enjoyed by the students of the Creative Chinese Cooking Class. The class has been conducted under the auspices of the Continuing Education Department of Ann Arbor Public Schools. The utensils and ingredients, for the most part, can be found in

American kitchens and supermarkets.

Good food does more than fill our stomachs. Good food can make us feel like a whole person. It can bring to life our keen anticipation for the future and change our attitudes toward our daily work. It also can evoke our sweet memory of the past. Its preparation can be seen as an act of love, of self-fulfillment, of creativity and of relatedness. Enjoying good food with loved ones can give us a sense of communion and stimulate a deepening and enrichment of friendship. But above all, let us not neglect the spiritual aspect of life. For the Bible says "Man shall not live by bread alone, but by every word that proceeds from the mouth of God" (Matt. 4:4). While we enjoy a good dinner, let us remind ourselves, it is out of His bountifulness and His presence we derive every bit of our enjoyment.

Here is the book, sincerely I present it to you. I have tried to make the recipes simple, practical, economical and nutritious and yet retain all the authentic flavor. As an American trained nutritionist of Chinese background and as a U.S. citizen, I hope this unique book will be a small cultural contribution to this great melting pot society, especially in this year of the bicentennial celebration of our nation. It is also my earnest desire that this book will bring to you and your family many occasions of happiness, meaningful experiences and health.

Is Chinese Food Nutritious?

A. THE PROTEIN FACTS

Since the Chinese people use less meat and more vegetables in their cooking, many students and friends asked me if Chinese food is nutritious enough. The answer, fortunately, is a very definite yes.

First of all, let us find out, based on nutrition science, why we need to eat meat and why it is so important. Meat provides us with protein of high biological value. Biochemically, protein from the muscles of animals is closely related to protein of man.

Proteins are the basic materials of our bodies. Protein, in turn, is made of a large number of amino acids which are called building blocks. The body proteins are made of about 20 amino acids; eight of them are not synthesized by the body in sufficient amounts. These are called "essential" amino acids. They must be supplied in the diet. The other twelve can be formed from other amino acids and carbohydrate residues, if enough food is consumed. With these building blocks, the body can manufacture thousands of proteins for various parts of the body. Some proteins are small; others are large.

When we eat protein food, the alimentary tract with its fluids digests the protein into amino acids which are absorbed through the intestinal lining into the blood and are carried to every part of the body. There, they are used for growth or rebuilding some of the proteins which are constantly broken down.

A protein of high biological value (or protein of good quality) is that which provides essential amino acids in the proportions that will meet our needs. The essential amino acids must be present simultaneously while the body manufactures protein. We do not have to get our good quality protein from meat alone. Besides beef and pork, poultry, fish, cheese and eggs all provide good quality proteins. One ounce of each of these foods contains, on the average, 7 grams of protein.

A protein of lower biological value (or protein of poor quality) is one which has a more unfavorable distribution of amino acids, especially essential amino acids. We have to eat more of it in order to get enough of essential amino acids we need. Consequently, we have a number of amino acids left over to dispose of. The proteins of rice, wheat, oats, corn, gelatin, fruit and vegetables generally belong to this class.

When we mix various proteins from different foods, the overall result will be better than what could be anticipated from each of the constituents. One food may be high in the amino acids missing in another. The proteins from several foods may complement each other.

Chinese food is a perfect example of such mutual complementation of proteins. While cooking Chinese food, we use a variety of vegetables with a small quantity of meat (or other food of animal source) so that the shortage of amino acids in one food is supplemented by amino acids contained in others. The mixture of proteins from different sources increases the total protein value. The essential amino acids contained in the small quantity of meat extends its highest effectiveness.

USDA estimates that the average American eats more protein than his body can use, from ten to twelve percent more. The Recommended Dietary Allowances for the adults are 55 - 65 grams daily. The meat consumption in the U.S.A. in the last decades has risen about fifty percent. All we need, in order to be well fed, is a protein mixture yielding enough amino acids in the right proportion.

B. OTHER ADVANTAGES

Eating less meat reduces the saturated fat and cholesterol in the diet. This is particularly important for the people who have to watch their cholesterol intake.

Fats, like other foods, are readily digested by the normal person into fatty acids which are utilized by the body as part of its constituents or as a source of energy. There are several kinds of fatty acids, namely, saturated fatty acids, unsaturated fatty acids and polyunsaturated fatty acids. The saturated fatty acids are found chiefly in animal fats. The other kinds, unsaturated and polyunsaturated fatty acids, are found chiefly in vegetable oil (except coconut oil). Cholesterol is a fatty substance generally associated with foods of animal origin, especially animal fat. It does not appear in vegetable foods.

The diet high in saturated fat promotes elevation of the level of cholesterol in the blood and therefore increases the risk of coronaries and other diseases of the heart and blood vessels. Lowering meat intake will automatically lower the intake of saturated fat and cholesterol in a diet.

The Chinese method of cooking vegetables is also beneficial for the health from the nutritional standpoint. Vegetables are usually stir-fried with a little vegetable oil and a small amount of water over high heat. The vegetables stay crisp after cooking and the full value of the vitamins and minerals are retained. Besides, when the dishes are cooked with a large portion of vegetables, the overall calorie content is lower than the Western-style dishes.

A well planned Chinese meal is not only nutritious but healthful and after all, remaining healthy is the basic reason for eating. Chinese food provides an interesting and welcome change to the typical Western diet.

About Monosodium Glutamate (MSG)

MSG has received a lot of publicity since 1968. People are very confused about its nature and what it does to food. In this section, I have tried to examine the available scientific information about MSG and tried to draw a tentative conclusion from that information. Hopefully, it will help to clarify some misunderstandings about its use.

A. THE FIRST IMPRESSION:

My first experience with MSG in enhancing food flavor occurred shortly after college graduation. I was invited by one of my schoolmates to have dinner in her home. All the dishes served were very delicious, even the simplest. We knew she was not an especially good cook. Out of appreciation and curiosity, I asked her what she had done to make the meal turn out so well. She told me that she put a little MSG in every dish she cooked to improve the flavor.

B. WHAT IS MSG?

MSG is a flavor enhancer, a food additive. It is one of the approximately five hundred food additives currently used. It is the sodium salt of glutamic acid, an amino acid that has a meaty flavor. Glutamic acid is one of the building blocks of which protein molecules are made and is present in all protein foods.

MSG was first discovered by a German scientist in the late eighteenth century. In 1908 Dr. Kikunae Ikeda, a chemist at Tokyo University, was the first person to discover the ability of MSG to intensify the flavor of foods. Since then, it has been produced commercially either from bacterial fermentation of sugar or from plant proteins in great quantity.

An incident which first indicated that MSG did something other than enhance the flavor of food occurred in 1968. A Chinese doctor, Dr. Kwork, reported that about 20-30 minutes after beginning a meal at a Chinese restaurant, he experienced a burning sensation in the back of his neck and in his forearms, tightness of the chest and headaches. The name, "Chinese Restaurant Syndrom (CRS)," was coined to describe these symptoms.

Later on, several New York doctors followed up Dr. Kwork's observations by eating a wide variety of dishes at their favorite Chinese restaurants. Some of them experienced Dr. Kwork's symptoms. They traced the cause to the soup. The cook usually added a large quantity of MSG to the soup, (as high as 3.5 grams per serving which is about ⅔ teaspoon) and the soup is usually the first course of a meal. When a large amount of MSG in the soup enters the empty stomach, it is readily and completely absorbed into the blood which carries it to the nerve endings where it probably exerts its effects. The sensitivity is different from person to person.

Since then, scientists have carried out numerous experiments by feeding and injecting different levels of doses of MSG to different species and age groups of animals to study the toxicity of this chemical. Up to this date anatomical studies on newborn and infant animals treated with large doses revealed damages to the brain and the retina of the eyes. Death would occur to day-old chicks when subcutaneously treated with 5 gm/kg of MSG. Five grams per kilograms of body weight is indeed high as compared to the body weight of the chicks. No brain damage or other harm has been observed during the studies on adult rabbits and chickens given doses as high as 2.5 grams per kilogram of body weight each day.

The effects of feeding MSG to man have been investigated under a variety of circumstances and dosages. In general, these studies have produced no evidence of overt toxicity. The so-called Chinese Restaurant Syndrome represents a normal pharmacologic response to a rapid increase in plasma levels of glutamic acid, according to Prof. Dr. G.N. Wogan of MIT (*Report On Monosodium Glutamate*, Sept. 6, 1971).

Biochemical studies of MSG on adult mice recently conducted by Creasey and Malawista indicated the MSG interference with glucose intake by brain tissue. The interference is dose-related (300 mg and 600 mg by intraperitoneal injection). This study is probably an additional explanation of the CRS symptom.

C. SHOULD WE USE MSG?

The toxicity of MSG has not been fully studied. No standard of safety has been set. Infants should not be fed any amount of MSG

8

(or any other food additives). The development of the brain cells and other organs are critical to the infant. Any artificial chemicals should be excluded from their diet. Pregnant women should also be very careful about consuming MSG. Those who must restrict their salt intake should also restrict their MSG intake.

People around the world commonly use MSG to enhance the flavor of soup, meat, seafood, poultry, sauces or even cheese. Many food manufacturers and restaurants (especially Oriental ones) use MSG to intensify the meaty flavor of a food. If you check the ingredients of canned meat products, soup or soup mixes, TV dinners and many others, you will find that there are few products which do not include MSG. If it is not MSG per se listed in the ingredients, there will be the so-called "flavoring." For example, the imitation chicken and beef "flavoring" contains hydrolyzed vegetable protein, sugar, vegetable fat, amino acids, sodium inosinate, disodium quanylate, modified starch and "MSG," which is collectively called "flavoring."

I personally am not in favor of using MSG in everyday cooking. But its occasional use in small quantities to make food more palatable and to stir up the appetite will not do any harm. This is my personal view until scientists prove that it should be otherwise. In this book I suggest that the maximum amount of MSG for any recipe be not more than 1/8 teaspoon (about 0.6 gm) or even less. If too much MSG is used, the MSG flavor becomes dominant, and consequently loses its proper function.

I often give my students the following advice. When you invite friends to have a Chinese dinner in your home, do not forget to put some MSG in the dishes you are going to serve. MSG added will definitely enhance the flavor of the food. Use it when you serve home-made Chinese food occasionally for your family. I feel that since this is only once in a while, it will not do any harm. On the other hand, by so doing, you secure confidence in your cooking and you make your food more delicious and your friends and family happier.

If you cook Chinese food every day the situation is different. Using MSG on a daily basis is not a commendable practice. You should exercise discipline and judgment in each and every occasion.

Custom, Chopsticks and Tea

Mealtimes are very important events in the day of the Chinese family. Mealtime is family union time. The children should be present at the dinner table. Mothers try to do their best to make several palatable dishes, even though the materials may be limited.

Most Chinese are very hospitable. They love to entertain people and share good meals with their friends. Food and friendship are inseparable in China. Any gathering without food is considered incomplete and improper.

Rice is the popular staple of southern and middle parts of China. However, people in the northern part of China prefer wheat as their staple grain.

Foods are served with chopsticks and spoons. Fingers are not allowed for picking up foods. The Chinese consider using the fingers to eat as bad manners and barbarous behavior. Chopsticks are made of bamboo, wood, plastic, ivory, silver or gold. They are usually square at the top and tapered slightly at the end to pick up the food.

It is slightly difficult to handle the chopsticks at first. But with a little practice you will quickly manage them.

To use them:

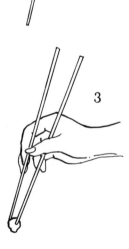

(1) Hold one of the chopsticks like a pencil, between the tips of thumb, index and middle fingers.

(2) Rest the upper part of the other stick at the base of your thumb and index fingers. The lower part of this stick rests on the tip of the ring finger and the first part of the small finger's back.

(3) Move the stick that is being held like a pencil in an up-and-down motion to meet the tip of the other stick. Food will be picked up and held between the tips of the two chopsticks.

Tea plays an important role in Chinese society. It is taken by all kinds of people in many kinds of ways. It is the beverage of the nation. Tea is served with meals or after meals. Guests or visitors are always offered a cup of tea, with or without some sweet tidbits, regardless of the time of day or night. Tea is often prepared in the home and is served in business offices, at ceremonial occasions and at social gatherings. It serves as a social beverage, somewhat like coffee in the United States.

There are hundreds of varieties of tea in China. Each kind has its own distinctive flavor. People outside China generally prefer the scented flower teas, such as jasmine tea or rose tea. Try some different ones and find out which kind you and your family like best. It might give you a series of adventures, surprises and pleasures. As a rule, the Chinese drink plain tea without adding cream or sugar. By drinking it this way they feel the delicate flavor of the tea will not be disturbed. Imagine if tea lovers like the Chinese put cream and sugar in every cup of tea they drink, how many extra calories and cholesterol they would get!!

How to make tea? First put the tea leaves in a pot (or cup), then pour in boiling water. Cover the pot and let the tea leaves steep for 3-5 minutes. The quantity of tea leaves used depends upon the freshness and quality of the tea, the effects desired from drinking the tea and of course, personal taste. Use fewer leaves when the tea is very fresh or of very high quality. Strong tea stimulates both mind and spirit. Light tea refreshes and relaxes. As a rule of thumb, one level teaspoonful of tea leaves will make a cup of very good tea and will usually allow for a refill (recipe on page 259).

At a Chinese feast the guests are seated shortly after they arrive. The guest of honor sits facing the door while the host and hostess sit opposite him. Each table, usually round, seats from eight to twelve persons.

Traditional Chinese-style feasts are very complicated. They usually start with four to six cold dishes and continue through eight to sixteen main dishes. These dishes are served one or two at a time; somewhere in between the main courses, two sweet dishes are served. The rice and soup are usually served when the main courses are almost finished.

A simple family meal for six people would include one soup placed in the center of the table and surrounded by four main dishes. Two of the main dishes would be heavy meat dishes containing more meat than vegetables. The other two would be light meat dishes, in which the proportion would be reversed. Those delicious dishes are shared by the diners with a separate bowl of rice. Each person serves himself. Chinese people seldom count how many helpings they consume at each meal, so guests do not feel selfconscious if they take extra portions of a favorite dish.

In China, people do not serve heavy appetizers. Instead, a cup of plain tea accompanied by roasted watermelon, pumpkin seeds in shells, or a few kinds of delicate fruit preserves might be served. These delicacies tend to create an atmosphere of relaxation but not kill the appetite as heavy appetizers do. The cold dishes are the Chinese equivalent of Western-style appetizers.

It is perfectly all right to serve your Chinese dinner in the American way, that is, to serve some appetizers before dinner. This book contains several recipes which could be served as appetizers as well as main dishes (see the Recipe Index, page 314).

The busy American lifestyle makes it impossible to cook and serve as many dishes as the Chinese might. However, a meal of only a few dishes made with careful planning, imagination, and artistic arrangement can be both successful and enjoyable.

祝

您

健

康

Method of Preparation and Cooking

The way in which ingredients for Chinese cooking are cut, sliced, chopped etc. is very important, not only from an aesthetic point of view (which should be a primary consideration) but from the point of view of consistency of cooking time for the various ingredients. Because Chinese food is, for the most part, prepared for fast cooking over high heat, the ingredients must be uniform in size so that they will all be done at the same time.

A. PREPARATION:

Mince: To cut into very fine pieces.

Chop: To cut into small pieces without concern for the shape.

Dice: To cut into ¼"-½" cubes.

Cube: To cut into 1" cubes.

Chunk: To cut into 2" cubes.

Crush: To increase the exposed surface by pounding with the broad side of a cleaver or knife.

Slice: To cut into thin, flat pieces about 1½" long, 1" wide and 1/8" thick.

Slant-slice: To increase the exposed surface by putting the article 45 degrees to your cleaver or knife, and slice it into thin pieces. Asparagus, carrots and similar vegetables are usually cut in this way.

Shred: Slice the article first then pile a few pieces together and cut into fine strips.

Rolling-cut: Slant slice first, then turn the cut surface upward, and slant slice again at the end of the first cut surface.

Marinate: To soak and mix the article in a seasoned sauce to improve its flavor.

B. COOKING:

Braising: To brown quickly and then cook long and slowly in a tightly covered pan until the food is done.

Stir-frying or sautéeing: Use little oil; the food is stirred and turned frequently during cooking. This is the most popular method of Chinese cooking.

Pan-frying: Use enough oil to barely cover the food to be fried. Food may be turned once or twice while cooking.

Deep-frying: Use at least one cup of oil. The food is cooked by immersing in hot oil (375° - 400°) until done.

Boiling: Cook food in boiling water until done.

Simmering: Bring the food to a boil first, then turn to low heat with the lid on; cook until the food becomes tender or done.

Steaming: Expose the food directly to the action of steam. It usually takes much less fuel to steam food than roasting or baking.

Cooking Utensils

It is not absolutely necessary to buy special utensils in order to cook Chinese food. However, there are a few items which are indispensable in order to cook Chinese food efficiently and to secure the best result.

Cleaver: This is an all-purpose, rectangular-shaped knife. You can use it to cut all types and shapes of meat and vegetables. There are several sizes but the smallest one (7½" x 3½") is the best size for the American kitchen. But any kind of broad shaped knife is acceptable.

Cutting board: A large cutting board is necessary because it is heavy and sturdy. A large board is also convenient because it has room on which to store the ingredients after they are cut thus eliminating the need for extra dishes. When the cutting is completed, the board can be carried to the stove and the ingredients cooked one by one.

Teflon-coated fry pan or any other kind of non-stick pan: stickiness is the worst part of Chinese cooking. A teflon or non-stick frying pan will solve this problem. Teflon and non-stick frying pans are available in hardware stores, department stores and some supermarkets.

Large deep *sauce pan* or *Dutch oven:* This is used for boiling noodles and other foods. The pan can also be used as a temporary steamer.

Medium sauce pan: Use this pan for food requiring slow cooking or simmering.

Wok: This is an all-purpose Chinese cooking pan designed especially for the Chinese stove. It is not absolutely necessary for authentic Chinese cooking in the United States. The wok is very good for deep frying food because it has a narrow, round bottom and wide sloping sides so that it needs less oil than a regular pan. The wok is also very good for stir-frying vegetables.

Steamer: Nearly all the families in China own one or more sets of steamers but an oven is rare. Most of the steamers were made of bamboo years ago. Metal steamers are becoming more popular since they last longer and are easier to keep clean.

A complete steamer contains a base, which is a large sauce pan (the wok serves as base for the bamboo steamer), 2-4 tiers of perforated pans, and a cover.

When steaming food: (1) Fill the pan about ⅓ full of water; cover and bring to a boil. (2) Remove the cover from the sauce pan. Set the tier with the food which is going to be steamed on the sauce pan. Put the cover on the tier and steam as the recipe requires. You can steam several dishes in separate tiers at once, saving both time and fuel.

You can make a temporary steamer from a large sauce pan or any kind of large deep pan. Just put a frame in the large pan and set the dish of the food on the frame. The frame can be made from 1-3 old tuna fish cans or fruit cans that have both ends removed. The cans are put into the pan of boiling water with a plate or dish containing the food to be steamed on top of the cans. Be sure the water level is 2 inches or more below the food being steamed so that the water is not boiled into the food. There should be enough space to allow the air to circulate freely. The pan should always be covered while steaming.

Menu Planning

When you plan a menu, there are several points you might bear in mind:

A. COLOR

People eat with their eyes as well as with their mouths. Choose dishes with a combination of different colors. Try to include bright, pale, dark and neutrally colored dishes so that the appearance of the whole dinner will be attractive and appetizing.

B. VARIETY

Do not repeat the same kind of meat in too many dishes. If you like to serve four dishes, for example, try to select from beef, pork, seafood and poultry, etc. When you only have one or two kinds of meat with which to cook several dishes, be sure to use different spices or different kinds of vegetables.

A carefully planned dinner would include dishes of various flavors: (bland, spicy), texture: (chewy or crunchy, soft or smooth), shapes: (whole pieces, carefully cut), in order to provide contrast and to reveal each dish's own character.

By planning this way, you add a greater measure of enjoyment and satisfaction to the dinner and also stimulate people's interest in different foods.

C. TIMING

Try to select the dishes that require different cooking techniques and time requirements such as braised, steamed, deep-fried, etc. Most braised dishes can be cooked weeks in advance and kept in the freezer. With such dishes, all you have to do is reheat and serve. There is no last minute work on most steamed dishes if you adjust the time correctly. Most deep-fried dishes can be reheated in the oven.

Many good dishes are stir-fry ones. They require a lot of cutting and preparation but few minutes of cooking. These dishes should be served the minute they are done and should be piping hot when brought to the table. When you entertain friends, be sure to limit stir-fry dishes to two or three. I further suggest that you cut and marinate all the meats a day in advance; cut all other ingredients hours in advance, wrap in plastic bags and keep them in the refrigerator until it is time to cook.

D. NUTRITION AND DIET

Good health through good nutrition and balanced diet should be one of the most important purposes of eating. The food we select should contain enough protein, carbohydrate, fat, vitamins and minerals. Water is also important but it is not within the scope of consideration in this book. The first three categories furnish the fuel or energy for our body which we call "calories." We need a certain amount of calories to sustain our lives. Vitamins and minerals are important for the vigor and vitality of our whole well-being. Lack of them will delay or affect the interaction and utilization of the other nutrients in the body. Fortunately, we need only a small amount of vitamins and minerals and they are abundantly supplied by a good variety of food. On the average, food from plants supply more than twice the amount of vitamins and minerals than meats.

Chinese cooking, as you see in this book, usually puts the meat and vegetables together in one dish. It is the most advantageous way of cooking with variety. Some dishes are almost a balanced diet in themselves.

For example:
1.) Fried noodles, soft type (see page 235)
The nutrition information of this recipe is:

Calories: 1660	Vitamin A: 11615 I.U.
Protein: 80gm	Thiamine (vit. B_1): 1.8mg
Fat: 84gm	Riboflavin (vit. B_2) 2.5mg
Carbohydrates: 145gm	Niacin: 27.25mg
Calcium: 0.7gm	Ascorbic acid (vit. C): 81mg
Iron: 15mg	

2.) Meat stuffed steamed buns (see page 275)
The nutrition information of this recipe is:

Calories: 2333 Vitamin A: 22433 I.U.
Protein: 112gm Thiamine (vit. B_1): 4.8mg
Fat: 127gm Riboflavin (vit. B_2): 0.2gm
Carbohydrates: 171gm Niacin: 28.5mg
Calcium: 0.6gm Ascorbic acid (vit. C): 94mg
Iron: 23.6mg

Compare the proportion of the nutrients of the two recipes with the daily requirements. See the table on page 303. We get almost all the necessary nutrients except calcium. To make up the calcium dificiency, we could add some calcium-rich food. This is not too difficult. There are many foods which are rich in calcium. The best and most convenient one is milk. One cup of milk will provide around 300 milligrams (0.3gm) of calcium.

Here are some other calcium-rich foods:

	Calories	Protein gm	Calcium mg
1 C whole milk	160	9	288
1 C skim milk	90	9	296
1 stalk of cooked broccoli	45	6	158
1 C of cooked collards	55	5	289
1 C of cooked turnip greens	30	3	525

These are just some samples. The important word is "variety." A variety of foods wisely chosen is the key to healthy eating.

It is important to be sure we are eating enough but not over-eating. We should check our own caloric need. When we eat too much, we take in more calories than the body needs. The body-system will convert the excessive calories into fat and the fat will be stored in the body as fat. Consequently, we gain weight.

I have endeavored to have nutrition information for each recipe. You will be able to decide and adjust the calories and nutrients
needed when you plan your own menu. I have tried to make the
nutrition information as complete and accurate as possible. However, certain foods such as wood ears, lily buds, Hoisin sauce, bean
threads, curry powder, Winter melon and sea cucumber have
never been analyzed for their nutritional value. Rather than not
give nutritional information for recipes containing these ingredients, I have calculated the information for these recipes with the
awareness that they cannot be completely accurate.

When you want to lose weight, all you have to do is to cut down
on calories. For an average adult to lose one pound of body fat, it
requires a loss of an approximate total of 3,500 calories. If you eat
500 calories less each day, within one week you would lose one
pound of body weight. If you try to cut 500 calories each day and
at the same time eat good and balanced food, you will not feel too
depressed. The same goal can be accomplished by doing a lot of
exercises while maintaining normal caloric intake.

To avoid cholesterol, I use vegetable oil in all the recipes. Also
the visible fat is removed from the meat before cooking to reduce
the calorie content of the food as well as minimize cholesterol.

If you are interested in more nutrition, read the section "Is
Chinese Food Nutritious?"

**NOTE: The Nutrition information following each recipe is the
calculation for the entire recipe, not for individual servings.**

E. MANAGEMENT

Planning and preparing a whole meal is pretty much a matter
of good management. Write down every thing you need to buy and
to do. Be sure to have all the necessary ingredients on hand and be
sure you understand all of the recipe directions. Find out which
steps of the recipe can be prepared in advance, what dish will be
served first, even which serving platters are going to be used.

When you give a dinner party for your friends, try to cook
dishes that you are most familiar with or you have tried before.

HERE ARE SIX SAMPLE MENUS FOR SIX TO TEN PEOPLE

1.
Cucumber soup (page 26)
Steamed black bean spareribs (page 79)
Braised shrimp in tomato sauce (page 145)
Beef with mushrooms (page 49)
Asparagus salad (page 179)
Rice (page 220) or Chinese steamed bread (page 238)
Almond bean curd (page 262)
Tea (page 259)

2.
Bean thread meat ball soup (page 31)
Braised beef (page 53)
Sweet and sour pork (page 87)
Lobster Cantonese style (page 154)
Broccoli Chinese style (page 167)
Rice (page 220) or Chinese steamed bread (page 238)
Almond cookies (page 270)
Tea (page 259)

3.
Egg drop soup (page 24)
Asparagus with beef (page 42)
Braised pork hock or pork shoulder (page 82)
Fish fillet with tomato sauce (page 139)
Stir-fry Bok Choy (page 166)
Rice (page 220) or Chinese steamed bread (page 238)
Banana in mink coat (page 264)
Tea (page 259)

4.
Hot and sour To Fu soup (page 211)
Chicken and nuts (page 111)
Lion's head (page 93)
Braised shrimp in tomato sauce (page 145)
Broccoli Chinese style (page 167)
Rice (page 220) or Chinese steamed bread (page 238)
Fresh fruits
Tea (page 259)

5.
Wonton soup (page 34)
Black bean chicken (page 97)
Beef with mushrooms (page 49)
Shrimp with green peas and tomato (page 147)
Asparagus salad (page 179)
Rice (page 220) or Chinese steamed bread (page 238)
Black beauty (page 266)
Tea (page 259)

6.
Velvet corn soup (page 25)
Pearl meat balls (page 69)
Chicken breast with Hoisin sauce (page 114)
Sweet and sour spareribs (page 80)
Broccoli Chinese style (page 167)
Rice (page 220) or Chinese steamed bread (page 238)
Sesame seed candy (page 260)
Tea (page 259)

Six additional menus given on pages 315-318 have been evaluated in terms of specific nutrients. They are well balanced meals designed for people "on diets" or those who want "to watch their diets."

soups

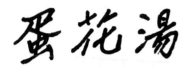

EGG DROP SOUP
(Dan Hua Tang)

Ingredients:

    2 eggs, beaten
    3 chicken bouillon cubes
    3 C water
    1 green onion, minced
    1 T cornstarch blended with ¼ cup of water
    1 t sesame oil

Method:

1. Put the chicken bouillon cubes and water in a sauce pan; bring to a boil.

2. Stir in blended cornstarch; then stir in eggs. Remove from heat immediately.

3. Sprinkle minced onion and sesame oil on the surface of the soup.

Serve hot.

Makes 4 servings
Time: 8 minutes

Calories: 249
Protein: 15 gm

Carbohydrates: 8gm
Fat: 17gm

VELVET CORN SOUP
(Su Mi Tang)

Ingredients:

    10 oz frozen cut corn thawed, or corn from fresh
        ears
     3 C water
     4 chicken bouillon cubes
     1 C milk
     2 T cornstarch dissolved in ¼ C water
     2 egg whites
     2 T minced ham (about 1 oz.)
     1 green onion, minced
        Salt and pepper to taste

Method:

1. Beat the egg white lightly. Set aside.
2. Put corn, water and chicken bouillon cubes in a blender; blend for 1 minute.
3. Pour the corn mixture in a sauce pan; add milk and bring to a boil.
4. Add dissolved cornstarch stirring constantly until the soup thickens.
5. Remove from heat; fold in egg white.
6. Pour in a tureen. Sprinkle minced onion, ham and a little pepper on the surface of the soup. Serve hot.

One half to one teaspoon of sesame oil can be added before serving.

Makes 6 servings
Time: 10 minutes

Calories: 585   Carbohydrates: 82 gm
Protein: 33 gm   Fat: 17gm

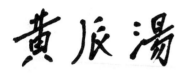

CUCUMBER SOUP
(Huang Gua Tang)

Ingredients:

¼ lb pork, sliced into 1½" long x ½" wide x
1/6" thick pieces
1 T soy sauce
1/8 t pepper
1 thin slice of fresh ginger
1 t cornstarch
1 cucumber
4 C water
3 chicken or beef bouillon cubes
1 green onion, minced
1 t sesame oil

Method:

1. Mix sliced pork with the next four ingredients.
2. Peel cucumber; split into two halves. Use a spoon to discard the seedy portion then cut the cucumber into slices.
3. Put water and bouillon cubes in a sauce pan and bring to a boil.
4. Add cucumber slices and bring to a boil.
5. Add meat slices one by one; bring to a boil again.
6. Reduce heat to medium and cook for 5 minutes. Pour the soup in a tureen. Sprinkle with sesame oil and minced onion. Serve hot.

Step 1 of the "Method" (meat) can be prepared in advance.

Makes 6 servings
Time: 20 minutes

Calories: 394
Protein: 25 gm

Carbohydrates: 12 gm
Fat: 27 gm

PICKLED MUSTARD GREEN SOUP
(Xian Cai Tang)

Ingredients:

    ¼ lb shredded pork or chicken breast
    1 T soy sauce
    ¼ t pepper
    ¼ t onion powder
    1 t cornstarch
    ½ C shredded bamboo shoots
    ⅓ recipe (about ½ cup) of pickled mustard greens,
        minced (see page 183)
    3 C water
    2 chicken bouillon cubes
    1 t sesame oil

Method:

1. Mix meat shreds with the next four ingredients.
2. Put the bouillon cubes and water in a medium sauce pan and bring to a boil. Be sure the bouillon cubes are dissolved.
3. Add meat shreds (a few each time so they will not stick together) and bamboo shoots. Bring to a boil.
4. Add mustard greens and sesame oil. Bring to a boil. Serve hot.

The meat part (step 1 of the "Method") can be prepared in advance.

Makes 4-6 servings
Time: 20 minutes

Calories: 392
Protein: 25 gm

Carbohydrates: 11 gm
Fat: 27 gm

(Calculated with pork butt)

麻油雞湯

**SESAME FLAVORED
CHICKEN SOUP**
(Ma You Ji Tang)

Ingredients:

½ chicken (about 1 pound)
1 T sesame oil
6 slices of ginger root
2 green onions, shredded
¼ C sherry
3 C water
1 t salt
¼ t pepper

Method:

1. Cut chicken into bite size, 1½" cubes.
2. Heat sesame oil in a deep sauce pan. Sauté ginger and onion. Add chicken; stir-fry for 2 minutes.
3. Add sherry and bring to a boil.
4. Add water. Bring to a boil; turn to low heat and simmer for 30 minutes. Sprinkle pepper over the soup before serving. Serve hot.

Makes 4-6 servings
Time: 35 minutes

Calories: 561
Protein: 57gm

Carbohydrates: 4 gm
Fat: 29gm

WINTER MELON SOUP
(Dong Gua Tang)

Ingredients:

- 1 lb Winter melon
- ½ lb ham (Smithfield or Todd's Old Virginia) sliced into 2" x ½" x 1/16" slices
- 4 dried mushrooms, soaked and sliced
- ½ C bamboo shoots, cut into 2" x ½" x 1/8" slices
- 1 green onion, shredded
- 2 thin slices of ginger root
- 5 C water
- 4 chicken bouillon cubes
- 1 t sesame oil
  Salt and pepper to taste

Method:

1. Wash and cut off the green skin of the melon. Discard the seedy portion and cut melon into ½" thick pieces.
2. Have the bamboo shoots, ham, ginger root slices, mushroom slices and green onion shreds ready.
3. Put all the ingredients, except sesame oil in a sauce pan. Cover and bring to a boil.
4. Turn to low heat and simmer for 20 to 30 minutes. Add sesame oil. Serve hot.

Makes 6-8 servings
Time: 20-30 minutes

Calories: 805
Protein: 50 gm

Carbohydrates: 9 gm
Fat: 60 gm

蝦米粉絲湯 BEAN THREAD AND DRIED SHRIMP SOUP
(Xia Mi Fen Si Tang)

Ingredients:

- 4 T dried shrimp (about 50 grams)
- 2 oz bean thread
- 5 C water
- 4 C chicken consommé or broth
- 1 green onion, shredded
- 4 thin slices of ginger root
- 1 lb celery cabbage, shredded
- 1 T oil
- Few drops of sesame oil

Method:

1. Heat oil in a deep sauce pan. Sauté onion and ginger root.

2. Add water, chicken broth, bean thread and dried shrimp; cover pan and bring to a boil.

3. Turn to low heat; simmer for 30 minutes.

4. Add shredded cabbage. Cook over medium heat for 5 minutes.

5. Add a few drops of sesame oil before serving. Serve hot.

This dish does not require constant attention while cooking.

Makes 4-6 servings
Time: 35 minutes

Calories: 517   Carbohydrates: 28 gm
Protein: 62 gm   Fat: 18 gm

(See page 20)

BEAN THREAD AND MEAT BALL SOUP
(Xian Fen Rou Wan Tang)

Ingredients:

2 oz bean thread
½ lb ground pork or beef
1/8 t onion powder or 1 T minced onion
1/8 t pepper
½ t salt
1 t soy sauce
1 t minced ginger root
1/8 t MSG (optional)
3 C water
3 C chicken broth or consommé
½ lb sliced celery cabbage

For garnishing (optional)
1 green onion, minced
2 T minced egg shreds (optional, recipe on page 242)

Method:

1. Soak bean thread in warm water for 20 to 30 minutes; drain.

2. Mix the meat with the next six ingredients. Form into ½" meat balls. (Use teaspoon to make meat balls).

3. Boil 3 cups of water in a sauce pan. Drop meat balls one by one into the water. Cook 10 minutes over medium heat. Discard fat from the surface of the soup.

4. Cut bean thread into 2-3" lengths. Add bean thread and chicken broth to the meat ball soup. Cook for 5 minutes.

5. Add cabbage; cook for 2 minutes. Garnish with minced onion and egg shreds before serving. (cont'd)

One half to one teaspoon of sesame oil can be added before serving.

The cooked meat balls can be refrigerated or frozen. Re-heat them before using.

Dried bean thread is sold in Oriental grocery stores or in supermarkets.

Makes 6 servings
Time: 20 minutes

Calories: 741   Carbohydrates: 12gm
Protein: 59 gm   Fat: 48gm

(Calculated with ground pork butt, also see page 20)

**NOODLE SOUP WITH
ASSORTED VEGETABLES**
(Shi Jin Mian Tang)

Ingredients:

  ½ lb thin spaghetti noodles or 1 pound fresh
     Chinese noodles (recipe on page 231)
  1 T dried black wood ears
 20 lily buds
  ½ C bamboo shoot slices
  2 eggs, beaten with a little salt
  ¼ lb pork loin or beef flank steak
  1 T soy sauce
  1 t cornstarch
  6 5/8" bouillon cubes in 5 cups of water, or 5 cups
     of chicken broth (If you use beef, then change to
     beef bouillon cubes.)   (*cont'd*)

2 green onions, shredded
2 slices of ginger root
¼ t pepper
¼ lb fresh spinach leaves
1 t sesame oil
1 T cornstarch blended with ¼ C of water
4 T oil

Method:

1. Soak lily buds in hot water for 10 minutes. Drain and remove stems; tie into knots. (See page 212).

2. Soak wood ears in hot water for 10 minutes; wash and drain.

3. Slice the meat into 1" x 2" x 1/6" slices. Mix with soy sauce and cornstarch.

4. Add spaghetti to 2-3 qt. of rapidly boiling water. Add 1 T salt to the water; cook for 10 minutes. (If fresh Chinese noodles are used, cook for 5 minutes only). Drain and rinse thoroughly with cold water.

5. Heat oil in a non-stick pan; sauté green onions and ginger root. Add meat; stir-fry until the color turns. Add lily buds, wood ears and pepper; mix well. Set aside.

6. Put the bouillon cubes and water in a deep sauce pan, bring to a boil. Stir in blended cornstarch, egg and cooked noodles; bring to a boil. Remove from heat; add spinach and sesame oil.

7. Divide the noodle soup into six soup bowls. Add the meat mixture to each bowl. Serve hot.

Makes 6 servings
Time: 40 minutes

Calories: 1858   Carbohydrates: 193 gm
Protein: 72 gm   Fat: 90 gm

(Calculated with pork loin, also see page 20)

餛飩湯

Ingredients:

¼ lb ground pork
¼ lb shrimp, raw; or crab meat or lobster meat,
   minced
½ C bamboo shoots, minced
2 oz fresh mushrooms, minced or 2-3 dried
   mushrooms, soaked and minced
¼ onion, minced
1 t salt
1 t sherry
1 t minced ginger root
¼ t pepper
1/8 t MSG (optional)
1 large can of chicken broth
1 lb Wonton skins, about 70-80 pieces
½ C egg shreds (recipe on page 242)
3 green onions, minced

Method:

1. Combine the first ten ingredients; blend well. This will
be used as the Wonton filling.

2. Put ½ t of the filling in the center of the skin and fold it
up. (See sketches on page 289).

3. Boil 3 cups of chicken broth in a sauce pan. Add 20
Wontons. Cover the pan and bring to a boil.

4. Add ¾ C cold water; cover the pan and bring to a boil
once more.

5. Remove the pan from the heat and let the Wontons
remain in the pan, covered, for four minutes.

6. Divide the soup into 4 servings. Garnish with a little

minced onion and minced egg shreds; serve hot.

One half to one teaspoon of sesame oil may be added before serving.

Wonton filling can be prepared in advance. It can be kept in the refrigerator for a few days or in the freezer for weeks.

Wontons can be wrapped a few hours in advance. Arrange them on a floured tray and cover with foil. Keep refrigerated until ready to use.

Wrapped Wontons can be frozen.

To freeze Wontons: Arrange the well wrapped Wontons on a tray (uncovered) and keep in the freezer overnight. Carefully remove the frozen Wontons to a plastic bag; seal well and keep frozen. The Wontons do not need to be thawed before using.

See pages 286-7 on how to revive the dried Wonton skin.

Total calories of filling: 440
Total calories of one pound of Wonton skin: 920
Each Wonton contains approximately 18 calories.

Ingredients:

¾ C dried shark's fin (about 50 grams)
½ lb chicken breast
1 C bamboo shoots, shredded
4 medium size dried mushrooms, soaked and shredded
2 green onions, shredded
1 T finely shredded ginger root
4 C chicken broth
1 T soy sauce
1 t sherry
4 T cornstarch dissolved in ¼ C water
1 T oil
⅓ C ham (Smithfield or Todd's Old Virginia), finely shredded (about 2 oz.)
Salt, pepper and MSG to taste
Parsley leaves for garnishing
Few drops of sesame oil

Method:

1. Soak dried shark's fin in warm water for 4 hours.

2. Cook shark's fin with enough water to cover over medium heat, for 30 minutes. Let cool. Repeat the process until the shark's fin is softened (about 2-3 times). Rinse and drain.

3. Boil chicken breast with water in a covered sauce pan for 20 minutes over medium heat. Let cool. Tear the chicken breast with hands into fine shreds (discard skin and bone). Set aside.

4. Heat oil in a sauce pan. Sauté onion and ginger. Add chicken broth, shark's fin, chicken shreds, bamboo shoots,

(cont'd)

36

mushroom shreds, sherry, soy sauce and bring to a boil.

5. Add dissolved cornstarch; stir until the soup thickens. Add salt, pepper and MSG to taste.

6. Pour into a tureen. Shake a little pepper and a few drops of sesame oil on top. Put a few parsley leaves in the center, then spread the ham shreds around the green center. Serve immediately.

The soaked and cleaned shark's fin can be refrigerated or frozen.

Makes 6-8 servings

Calories: 995   Carbohydrates: 47 gm
Protein: 120 gm   Fat: 33 gm

BIRD'S NEST SOUP
(Yan Wo Tang)

燕窩湯

Ingredients:

- ½ C chicken breast, shredded (about ¼ pound)
- 1 T soy sauce
- 1 T sherry
- 1 t cornstarch
- ¾ C purified, dried, edible bird's nest (about 50 grams)
- ⅓ C ham (Smithfield or Todd's Old Virginia) (about 1/8 lb) thinly sliced
- 3-4 dried mushrooms, soaked and sliced
- ¼ C sliced bamboo shoots
- 4 C chicken broth
- 1 green onion, minced
- 1 T cornstarch blended with ¼ C cold water
  Salt and pepper to taste

(cont'd)

Method:

1. Mix chicken shreds with the next three ingredients. Set aside.
2. Soak the bird's nest in enough warm water to cover for 2-3 hours. Wash and drain.
3. Put the soaked bird's nest in a sauce pan. Add 4 cups cold water; bring to a boil. Reduce to low heat and simmer for 10 minutes. Drain, rinse and remove the tiny feathers from the nest. Wash and drain.
4. Put the bird's nest, chicken broth, mushrooms, bamboo shoots and ham in a sauce pan. Bring to a boil. Cook for five minutes on medium heat.
5. Add chicken shreds; bring to a boil.
6. Add well blended cornstarch; stir until the soup thickens. Pour the soup into a tureen. Sprinkle minced green onion on top. Serve hot.

Bird's nest can be purchased from Oriental grocery stores.

The soaked and washed bird's nest can be refrigerated or frozen.

Makes 6-8 servings

Calories: 375   Carbohydrates: 28 gm
Protein: 63 gm   Fat: 16 gm

The legend of the bird's nest soup:

The legend concerning the origin of the soup is very interesting. I will quote a paragraph from **Mary Sia's Cookbook**:

"This famous soup dates back to the thirteenth century when Genghis Khan and his Mongol hordes invaded China. The Sung emperor, retreating from one to the next, finally took refuge with his remaining followers on the tiny island of Yaishang. Unable to get food through the Mongol blockade,

(cont'd)

they were forced to live on any thing they could find, even the nest of swallows, which contained food that the parent birds had stored up for their young. Eventually the emperor gave up hope of retaining his throne and threw himself into the sea, to be followed by many of his court. Since then bird's nest soup has been served in memory of this fallen emperor."

The nest called for in the soup is the nest of a special sea swallow, found only in certain regions in China. That is why the soup is so special and expensive.

豆芽排骨湯

SPARERIBS SOUP WITH
SOY BEAN SPROUTS
(Dou Ya Bai Gu Tang)

Ingredients:

    1 lb lean spareribs, cut into bite size cubes
    4 slices of ginger root
    2 green onions, shredded
    1 T sherry
1½ t salt
1/8 t MSG (optional)
    5 C water
 ½ lb fresh soy beans sprouts

Methods:

1. Put the first seven ingredients in a deep sauce pan. Cover and bring to a boil. Lower heat and simmer for 40 minutes.
2. Add soy bean sprouts. Cover the simmer for 20 minutes Serve hot.
One half to one teaspoon of sesame oil can be added before serving.

Makes 6 servings
Time: 1 hour

Calories: 1224
Protein: 52gm

Carbohydrates: 14gm
Fat: 107gm

蘆筍牛肉

(Lu Sun Niu Rou)

Ingredients:

- 1 lb fresh asparagus
- ½ lb beef flank steak, sliced into 1½" x ½" x 1/8" slices
- 2 t sherry
- 1/8 t pepper
- 1/8 t onion powder
- 2 thin slices of ginger root
- 2 T soy sauce
- 1 T cornstarch
- ½ t salt
- ½ C water
- 1 t cornstarch blended with 1 T water
- 1 green onion, shredded
- 3 T oil

Method:

1. Wash and cut off the tough part of the asparagus, slant slicing into thin pieces.
2. Mix beef with next six ingredients.
3. Heat oil in a teflon pan. Stir-fry beef until color turns. Remove from heat. Place beef into a dish.
4. Add onion, asparagus and salt to the same pan and remaining oil; stir-fry for ½ minute.
5. Add water and blended cornstarch; cover pan and bring to a boil. Mix the cooked asparagus with cooked beef. Serve hot.

Step 2 of the "Method" can be prepared in advance.

One half to one teaspoon of sesame oil can be added before serving.

42

Makes 4-6 servings
Time: 35 minutes

Calories: 812　　　　　　　Carbohydrates: 25 gm
Protein: 58 gm　　　　　　Fat: 59 gm

**BEEF AND
STRING BEANS**
(Niu Rou Chao Se Ji Dou)　　牛肉炒四季豆

Ingredients:

　½　lb beef, shredded (flank, loin, round etc.)
　3　T soy sauce
　¼　t pepper
　1　t sherry
　½　t brown sugar
　1　T cornstarch
1/8　t MSG (optional)
　1　box (10 oz) French-cut frozen green beans, cut
　　　into 1" pieces
　½　small onion, shredded
　⅓　C water
　1　t cornstarch blended with 1 T of water
　4　T oil

Method:

1. Mix beef with 2 T soy sauce and the next five ingredients.
2. Heat oil in a non-stick pan. Distribute the beef evenly in the pan. Stir-fry beef until color turns (about 2-3 minutes). Remove cooked beef and set aside.
3. Use the same pan and remaining oil to sauté the onions.

(cont'd)

Add Beans, 1 T soy sauce, water, blended cornstarch, a pinch of pepper and MSG; bring to a boil.

4. Mix with cooked beef. Serve hot.

One half to one teaspoon of sesame oil can be added before serving.

Step 1 of the "Method" can be prepared in advance and can be refrigerated or frozen.

Makes 6 servings
Time: 20 minutes

Calories: 998   Carbohydrates: 33 gm
Protein: 58 gm   Fat: 68 gm

(Calculated with flank steak)

牛肉白菜

BEEF WITH BOK CHOY
(Niu Rou Bai Cai)

Ingredients:

   1 lb Bok Choy (a kind of Chinese cabbage, see page 311)
 ½ lb beef, sliced in 1"x1½"x¼" slices
  2 T soy sauce
  1 t sherry
 ¼ t pepper
1/8 t MSG
  1 T cornstarch
  1 green onion, cut into 2" lengths
2/3 t salt or to taste
 ½ C water
3-4 T oil

(cont'd)

Method:

1. Wash Bok Choy; cut into 1" long sections. Separate white sections from the green parts.
2. Mix beef with next five ingredients.
3. Heat oil in a non-stick pan. Add beef; stir-fry until color turns (1-2 minutes). Remove beef to a dish.
4. Sauté onion in the remaining oil. Add the white parts of the Bok Choy, ⅔ t salt; stir and mix for 1 minute.
5. Add ½ C water; cook for 2 minutes.
6. Add green parts of the Bok Choy. Stir and cook for 2 more minutes.
7. Add cooked beef; stir and mix well.
      Serve hot.
One half to one teaspoon of sesame oil can be added before serving.

Makes 6 servings
Time: 25 minutes

Calories: 806   Carbohydrates: 21 gm
Protein: 58 gm   Fat: 55 gm

(Calculated with beef flank steak)

青椒炒牛肉 **BEEF AND GREEN PEPPER**
(Jing Jiao Chao Niu Rou)

Ingredients:

1 lb beef flank steak, shredded
3 T soy sauce
¼ t pepper
¼ t onion powder
1 T cornstarch
1 large green pepper, shredded
2 green onions, shredded
1 t shredded ginger root
1 T soy sauce
3-4 T oil

Method:

1. Mix beef with the next four ingredients. Set aside.
2. Heat 2-3 T oil in a teflon pan. Stir-fry beef until color turns (2-3 minutes). Remove beef to a dish.
3. Add 1 T oil; saute onion and ginger. Add green pepper and 1 T soy sauce. Stir and cook for 2 minutes.
4. Add cooked meat; mix well. Serve hot.
Step 1 of the "Method" can be prepared in advance.

Makes 6 servings
Time: 35 minutes

Calories: 1124
Protein: 104 gm

Carbohydrates: 25 gm
Fat: 65 gm

BEEF AND BEAN SPROUTS
(Dou Ya Chao Niu Rou)

豆芽炒牛肉

Ingredients:

- ½ lb beef, shredded
- 1 T cornstarch
- 1½ T soy sauce
- ¼ t pepper
- ½ lb mung bean sprouts
- 2 green onions, shredded
- 1 t shredded ginger root
- ¼ t salt or to taste
- 1/8 t MSG (optional)
- 3 T oil

Method:

1. Mix beef with the next three ingredients.
2. Heat 2 T oil in a teflon pan. Stir-fry beef until color turns (about 1-2 minutes). Remove to a dish.
3. Add 1 T oil; brown onions and ginger root. Add bean sprouts, salt and MSG. Stir-fry until bean sprouts are wilted (about 1-2 minutes).
4. Add cooked beef. Mix well. Serve hot.

Shredded pork or chicken breast can be used and cooked in the same manner.

Makes 6 servings
Time: 20 minutes

Calories: 820   Carbohydrates: 24 gm
Protein: 59 gm   Fat: 54 gm

(Calculated with beef flank steak)

47

雪豆牛肉

SNOW PEAS WITH BEEF SLICES
(Xue Dou Niu Rou)

Ingredients:

- ¼ lb snow pea pods
- 1 lb beef, flank steak
- 4 T soy sauce
- ½ t onion powder
- ¼ t pepper
- 1 t sherry
- 1 T cornstarch
- 1 green onion, shredded
- ¼ C water
- 4 T oil
- 1 t cornstarch blended with 1 T water

Method:

1. Wash and snap off the stems and strings from both ends of the snow pea pods. Set aside.
2. Slice beef into the size of snow pea pods. Mix beef with 3 T of soy sauce and the next four ingredients. Set aside.
3. Heat 3 T oil in a teflon pan. Add beef; stir-fry until color turns. Remove and set aside.
4. Add 1 T oil to the same pan. Sauté the onion, add snow pea pods and 1 T soy sauce; stir and mix well (salt and pepper to taste).
5. Add ¼ C water and blended cornstarch, cover and bring to a boil. Add cooked beef; mix well. Serve hot.

One half to one teaspoon of sesame oil can be added before serving.

Step 2 of the "Method" can be prepared in advance.

Makes 6-8 servings

(cont'd)

Time: 35 minutes

Calories: 1250   Carbohydrates: 26 gm
Protein: 105 gm   Fat: 80 gm

BEEF WITH MUSHROOMS
(Dong Gu Niu Rou)

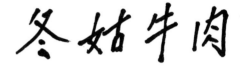

Ingredients:

    1 lb beef, sliced (flank, loin, round etc.)
    2 T soy sauce
1/8 t pepper
1/8 t MSG (optional)
    1 t sherry
 ½ t brown sugar
    1 T cornstarch
    1 green onion, shredded
    1 T cornstarch blended with 1/8 C of water
    4 T oil
      Salt and pepper to taste
 ½ lb fresh mushrooms, sliced
    1 C celery, sliced diagonally
 ¾ C water
    1 T soy sauce

Method:

    1. Mix beef with the next six ingredients.
    2. Heat oil in a teflon pan; sauté onion. Add beef; stir-fry until color turns (about 2 minutes). Remove.   (*cont'd*)

3. Put the last four ingredients into the pan; bring to a boil.

4. Add blended cornstarch and salt and pepper to taste. Cook until the sauce thickens.

5. Add cooked beef; mix well. Serve hot.

Step 1 of the "Method" can be prepared in advance. It can be kept in the refrigerator for a few days, or in the freezer for a few weeks.

Makes 6-8 servings
Time: 30 minutes

Calories: 1279   Carbohydrates: 27 gm
Protein: 107 gm   Fat: 80 gm

(Calculated with flank steak)

加厘牛肉

BEEF WITH CURRY
(Ka Li Niu Rou)

Ingredients:

    2 lb beef (boneless chuck, beef stew, loin ends or rib) cut into 1½" cubes

    1 onion, diced

 2-3 T curry powder mixed with 2 T water

    2 T soy sauce

    1 t salt

   ¼ t pepper

    2 C water

    2 medium size potatoes, peeled and cut with the rolling cut method

    1 T oil

(cont'd)

Method:

1. Heat oil in a medium sauce pan. Brown onion.
2. Add beef, curry paste, 2 T soy sauce, 1 t salt, ¼ t pepper and 2 C water; cover pan and bring to a boil.
3. Turn to low heat and simmer for 1½ hours.
4. Add potatoes, cook over medium heat for 20 minutes. If it is too dry, add a little water. Serve hot.

Potato pieces will be soft and broken. They will make a natural thick gravy of the dish.

This dish does not need special attention while cooking. Meat can be cooked in advance before adding potatoes. The leftovers can be reheated in a pan with a little water.

Makes 6-8 servings
Time: 2 hours

Calories: 2677   Carbohydrates: 49 gm
Protein: 177 gm   Fat: 192 gm

(Calculated with beef chuck. See page 20)

CHOW-CHOW BEEF
(Huo Che Kao Rou)

Ingredients:

    1 lb flank steak, round or chuck
    ½ t meat tenderizer
    2 T soy sauce
    1 t sherry
  2-3 T Hoisin sauce for dipping

(cont'd)

51

1 T sugar
1 T soy sauce
¼-½ t sesame oil
1 small can of "Sterno"

Method:

1. Cut the flank steak across the grain into 2"x1/6" slices.
2. Marinate the beef slices with the tenderizer, soy sauce and sherry for 1 hour.
3. Mix Hoisin sauce with next three ingredients and pour into a small saucer.
4. Grill the beef slices on small bamboo or metal skewers (about 5-6 inches long) over the Sterno flame for 1-2 minutes at the table. Dip the grilled beef in the Hoisin sauce before eating.

Calories: 713   Carbohydrates: 24 gm
Protein: 101 gm   Fat: 25 gm

(See page 20)

Sterno is sold in supermarkets. Read the directions carefully before using. It is a lot of fun for everyone at the table to cook his or her own meat.

BRAISED BEEF
(Hung Shao Niu Rou)

Ingredients:

- 3-4 lb boneless beef shank, beef chuck or beef stew, cubed
- 6 T soy sauce
- 2 green onions, cut into 2" lengths
- 6 thin slices of ginger root
- 3-4 whole star anise
- 1 T brown sugar
- 1 T oil

Method:

1. Cut beef into 1½" cubes or cook in whole piece.
2. Heat oil in a sauce pan. Sauté onion and ginger root for half a minute. Add beef and soy sauce. Stir and cook for 5 minutes.
3. Add 1½ C water and star anise; cover pan and bring to a boil.
4. Turn to low heat and simmer for 1 hour or until beef is tender.
5. Add brown sugar. Cook, uncovered, over high heat until water is almost evaporated. Serve hot.

This dish does not require constant attention while cooking. Any leftovers can be cooked with string beans, celery cabbage, turnips, spinach or wheat gluten.

The cooked meat can be refrigerated for a few days or frozen for a few weeks. Reheat the meat before serving.

Sliced cold braised beef can be served as appetizers, hors d'oeuvres and sandwich meat.

(cont'd)

Makes 6-8 servings
Time: 1½ hours

Calories: 4350   Carbohydrates: 21 gm
Protein: 243 gm   Fat: 358 gm

(Calculated with 3 pounds of beef chuck.)
    If the fat is discarded after cooking, the caloric content of this recipe will be reduced.

紅燒牛舌

BRAISED BEEF TONGUE
(Hung Shao Niu She)

Ingredients:

  1 beef tongue, 2-3 pounds
  3 green onions, halved
  1 inch ginger root, crushed
4-6 whole star anise
6-8 T soy sauce
  ¼ t thyme
  2 cinnamon sticks
  1 T brown sugar

(cont'd)

Method:

1. Fill a large deep sauce pan halfway with water. Bring to a boil.
2. Add beef tongue and cook for 6 minutes. Turn the tongue to other side and cook for 4 minutes more.
3. Remove tongue to a large platter; slit and peel off skin with a sharp knife. Wash and clean.
4. Put the cleaned tongue and all the remaining ingredients in a large sauce pan (if the beef tongue is too big, cut in half). Fill the sauce pan with water to 1" above the tongue. Cover pan and bring to a boil.
5. Reduce to low heat and simmer 2-3 hours or until the tongue becomes tender. If there is too much water left, increase heat and cook uncovered until water is almost evaporated. Turn the tongue from time to time while cooking.
6. Cut into thin slices before serving.
Serve hot or cold.
Sliced cold braised beef tongue can be served as hors d'oeuvres, appetizers, sandwich meat or as a cold dish.
It is easier to slice the beef tongue while cold.
It does not need constant attention while cooking.

Makes 10 servings
Time: 3 hours

Calories: 1313   Carbohydrates: 25 gm
Protein: 126 gm   Fat: 76 gm

(Calculated with 2 pounds of beef tongue)

炒心片　　　　　　　　**SAUTÉED BEEF HEART**
(Chao Xin Pian)

Ingredients:

½ lb beef or pork heart
3 T soy sauce
¼ t onion powder
¼ t pepper
1 T sherry
2 T cornstarch
1 C snow pea pods, about 100 gm
½ C water
1 t cornstarch dissolved in 1 T water
1/8 t MSG
2 green onions, shredded
3 thin slices of ginger root
3 T oil

Method:

1. Remove all the fat from the heart and cut it into thin pieces (the size of a snow pea pod).
2. Mix heart slices with 2 T soy sauce and the next four ingredients.
3. Clean the pea pods by snapping off both ends and strings.
4. Heat oil in a teflon pan. Sauté onions and ginger root. Add heart slices; stir-fry for 4 minutes or until no red liquid comes out from the heart slices. Remove to a dish.
5. Put water, snow pea pods and 1 T soy sauce into the pan and bring to a boil.
6. Add cornstarch and cooked heart. Mix well.
Serve hot.
One half to one teaspoon of sesame oil can be added before serving.
(cont'd)

Use string beans, Chinese cabbage or bamboo shoot slices as substitutes for snow pea pods if you wish.

Makes 6 servings
Time: 35 minutes

Calories: 811
Protein: 46 gm

Carbohydrates: 38 gm
Fat: 51 gm

(Calculated with beef heart)

DRIED BEEF SLICES
(Niu Rou Gan)

Ingredients:

  1 lb beef (flank, chuck or round), sliced in 1" x 2" x 1/6" slices
  1 C water
  1 T oil
  3 T soy sauce
  1 T sherry
  2 t minced ginger root
 ½ onion, minced
  2 whole star anise
  1 T brown sugar
 ¼ t five-spice powder
 ¼ t pepper
1-2 dried hot pepper (optional)

(cont'd)

Method:

1. Mix beef with the last nine ingredients. Marinate for one hour, stirring occasionally.
2. Place the beef slices in a sauce pan, add water, cover and bring to a boil.
3. Reduce to low heat and simmer for one hour.
4. Turn to high heat and cook until no juice remains.
5. Use 1 T oil to grease a tray. Transfer the cooked meat onto the tray. Bake the meat in a preheated 350° oven until dried. Serve cold.

Dried beef slices can be served as a snack. Mothers in China always like to make this kind of meat to send to their "away from home" children. It is much better than cookies and candies. The dried beef can be kept in the refrigerator for weeks without spoiling.

Calories: 840   Carbohydrates: 21 gm
Protein: 102 gm   Fat: 37 gm

(Calculated with beef flank steak)

SHREDDED BEEF CHOP SUEY
(Rou Si Shi Sui)

Ingredients:

- ½ lb beef flank steak, shredded
- 3 T soy sauce
- 1 T sherry
- ¼ t onion powder
- 3 slices of ginger root   (cont'd)

¼ t pepper
½ t brown sugar
1 t cornstarch
5 T oil
1½ C shredded celery
½ C shredded carrot
2-4 hot peppers, shredded (optional)
5 green onions, shredded
1 T soy sauce
Pinch of salt and pepper
1 t sesame oil

Method:

1. Marinate beef with the next six ingredients for 30 minutes. Coat the beef with cornstarch.

2. Heat 3 T of oil in a non-stick pan; stir-fry beef for 2 minutes then remove to a dish.

3. Put 2 T of oil in the pan and add the last seven ingredients; stir and mix for 5 minutes. Add cooked beef and mix well. Serve hot.

Makes 4-6 servings
Time: 25 minutes

Calories: 1100   Carbohydrates: 23 gm
Protein: 53 gm   Fat: 86 gm

洋葱牛肉

BEEF AND ONION
(Yang Cong Niu Rou)

Ingredients:

1 lb beef, sliced into 1½" x ½" x 1/8" slices (flank steak is preferred)
3 T soy sauce
¼ t pepper
1/8 t MSG (optional)
1 t sherry
¼ t brown sugar
2 T cornstarch
1 medium onion, chopped
⅓ C water
1 t cornstarch blended with 1 T water
3-4 T vegetable oil

Method:

1. Marinate beef with 2½ T soy sauce and the next five ingredients for ½ hour.
2. Heat oil in a non-stick pan. Spread beef evenly in the pan. Stir-fry beef until color turns (about 2 minutes). Do not overcook the beef. Remove cooked beef to a dish.
3. Use the same pan and remaining oil to sauté the onion with ½ T soy sauce and a pinch of salt, pepper and MSG. Add water and blended cornstarch. Bring to a boil.
4. Mix with cooked beef. Serve hot.

Step 1 of the "Method" can be prepared in advance and either refrigerated or frozen. The frozen beef should be thawed before using.

(cont'd)

Makes 4-6 servings
Time: 30 minutes

Calories: 1150
Protein: 102 gm

Carbohydrates: 31 gm
Fat: 75 gm

ANT NEST
(Ma Yi Shang Shu)

Ingredients:

    1 C ground beef (about ½ pound)
    2 T soy sauce
1/8 t MSG (optional)
    1 t sesame oil
1/8 t pepper
    2 t cornstarch
    1 small onion, minced
    1 T cornstarch blended with 2 T water
    2 oz dry bean thread
  ½ T oil
    Salt and pepper to taste
    Oil for deep-frying

(cont'd)

Method:

1. Mix beef with 1 T soy sauce and 2 t cornstarch.
2. Heat ½ T oil in a frying pan (meanwhile, heat oil in a deep sauce pan or wok for deep-frying bean thread). Brown onion; add beef and stir-fry until beef turns brown.
3. Add 1 T soy sauce, MSG, sesame oil, pepper and blended cornstarch. Bring to a boil (salt and pepper to taste).
4. Fry bean thread in 400° oil for a few seconds (it will expand quickly). Drain and arrange on a serving dish.
5. Pour hot meat sauce evenly over the fried bean thread. Serve hot.

This is a fast cooking dish. Prepare two pans to cook the meat and bean thread in at the same time.

Bean thread is also called cellophane noodles. They are made from ground mung beans and sold in half-pound or quarter-pound packages in Oriental grocery stores. They can be stored for a long time in a dry place.

Makes 6 servings
Time: 8 minutes

Calories: 780   Carbohydrates: 21 gm
Protein: 44 gm   Fat: 59 gm

(See page 20)

(Calculated with 4 T oil for deep-frying.)

STUFFED CUCUMBER
(Huang Gua Niang Rou)

Ingredients:

    3 medium-size cucumbers
   ½ lb ground pork or beef
    2 T dried shrimp (about 25 gm)
    8 water chestnuts, minced
    1 green onion, minced
    1 t minced ginger root
    1 T soy sauce
   ¼ t pepper
    1 t sherry
 1/8 t MSG (optional)
    1 green onion, cut into 2" lengths
    2 thin slices of ginger root
  ⅔ C water
    1 T soy sauce
    1 T oil

Method:

1. Soak dried shrimp in a small bowl with hot water for 1 hour. Drain and mince finely.

2. Wash and peel cucumbers; cut into 1½" sections. Use a small knife or teaspoon to remove seeds so that each section of the cucumber forms a ring.

3. Mix ground pork with the next eight ingredients.

4. Stuff the ground pork mixture in the holes of the cucumber rings.

5. Heat oil; brown both sides of the cucumber rings.

(cont'd)

6. Add water, 1 T soy sauce, ginger slices and green onion. Cover pan and bring to a boil. Reduce to low heat and simmer for 25 minutes or until the cucumbers are tender and only a few tablespoons of water remain. Serve hot. The leftovers can be reheated and served again.

Makes 6-8 servings
Time: 35 minutes

Calories: 887
Protein: 58 gm

Carbohydrates: 27 gm
Fat: 60 gm

(Calculated with ground pork butt)

STEAMED MEAT IN NOODLE CASE
(Shao Mai)

Ingredients:

- ½ lb ground pork or beef
- ½ C minced water chestnuts
- ¼ C minced onion
- ½ t salt
- 1 t sherry
- 1 t minced ginger root
- ¼ t pepper
- 3 dried mushrooms, soaked and minced
- 1/8 t MSG (optional)
- 2 T egg shreds, minced (see page 242)
- 2 green onions, minced (use the green parts of the onion)
- 2 T minced Virginia ham or Canadian ham (about 1 oz)
- 20 pieces of Wonton skin

(cont'd)

Method:

1. Combine the first nine ingredients; mix well. This will be used as the filling.

2. Place 1 heaping teaspoonful of filling in the center of a Wonton skin. Fold it up and form into a cylindrical shape. Pull out the edges of the skin a little to give it a "flower" appearance. Repeat with remainder of the Wonton skins.

3. Place them in an upright position in an oil-brushed tier of a steamer. Garnish the top of each noodle case with a few pieces of minced ham, green onion and minced egg shreds.

4. Steam 20 minutes. Serve hot.

If the steamed meat cases are made one or two days before serving, steam for 15 minutes only. Cool and keep in the refrigerator. Steam again for 10 minutes before serving.

Makes 20 meat cases.
Time: 30 minutes

Calories: 953
Protein: 53 gm

Carbohydrates: 55 gm
Fat: 55 gm

(Calculated with ground pork butt. Each meat case averages 47 calories)

麵筋釀肉

**MEAT STUFFED
WHEAT GLUTEN
(Mian Jing Niang Rou)**

Ingredients:

    1 C ground pork or beef (about ½ pound)
    1 green onion, minced
    2 thin slices of ginger root, minced
    6 water chestnuts, chopped
  1/8 t pepper
    2 T soy sauce
  1/8 t MSG (optional)
15-20 fried wheat gluten balls
    2 C water
   1½ T soy sauce
    1 t brown sugar

Method:

1. Mix the first seven ingredients together thoroughly.
2. Use your fingers to make an opening on the gluten balls.
3. Gently stick one of your fingers into the ball to make a space for stuffing the meat.
4. Put meat into the ball until almost full. Repeat the process until all the balls are stuffed with meat.
5. Put the meat balls, 2 C water, 1½ T soy sauce and 1 t brown sugar in a sauce pan. Cover and bring to a boil.
6. Turn to medium heat; cook until only a few tablespoons of water are left. Serve hot.

This dish can be prepared in advance. Reheat before serving. Celery cabbage may be added to cook with the gluten balls. Use about 1 pound of celery cabbage; cut into pieces 2" long and add to the pan at the end of the last step of the "Method." Cook until the cabbage becomes tender. Add a little salt or soy sauce if needed.

(cont'd)

Fried wheat glutens, also called vegetable steak, are sold in Oriental grocery stores or home made (page 186).

Makes 5-6 servings
Time: 30 minutes

Calories: 1184   Carbohydrates: 11 gm
Protein: 77 gm   Fat: 90 gm

(Calculated with ground beef)

STEAMED GROUND MEAT
(Zheng Rou Bing)

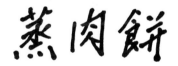

蒸肉餅

Ingredients:

  2 lb ground pork or beef
  3 medium size dried mushrooms, soaked and minced
  ½ C minced water chestnuts or bamboo shoots
  1 egg
  3 T soy sauce
  1 T sherry
  2 green onions, minced
  1 T minced ginger root
  ¼ t salt
  ¼ t pepper
  1/8 t MSG (optional)   *(cont'd)*

Method:

1. In a large bowl, thoroughly mix together all the ingredients.
2. Put the mixture in a deep, heat-proof bowl. Press flat on top.
3. Steam in a boiling steamer for 40 minutes.
4. Place the hot bowl with the meat in a cradle. Serve hot.

This dish does not require constant attention while cooking. Steamed meat can be reheated in a pan or in a steamer.

Step 1 of the "Method" can be prepared one or two days in advance. Keep in refrigerator until ready for steaming.

Makes 6-8 servings
Time: 40 minutes

Calories: 2420   Carbohydrates: 12 gm
Protein: 159 gm   Fat: 187 gm

(Calculated with ground pork butt)

PEARL MEAT BALLS
(Zhen Zhu Wan Zi)　　　珍珠丸子

Ingredients:

   1 C glutinous rice, about 200 grams
   1 lb ground pork or beef
 3-4 dried mushrooms, soaked and minced
  ¼ C water chestnuts, minced (about 6), or ¼ C minced bamboo shoots
   1 green onion, minced
   1 t minced ginger root
   1 egg
   2 t salt
   1 t sherry
 1/8 t pepper
 1/8 t MSG (optional)

Method:

1. Soak rice in cold water for 1 hour; rinse and drain well.
2. Mix pork with the next nine ingredients.
3. Form meat into 1½" diameter balls. Roll meat balls in rice until they are covered.
4. Grease a tier of a steamer. Arrange the meat balls on the greased tier. Be sure to allow a little space for the rice to expand.
5. Steam for 40-45 minutes. Serve hot.

Step 2 of the "Method" (without the rice) can be prepared in advance. The leftovers can be reheated by steaming for 10 minutes.

Glutinous rice, also called sweet rice, can be purchased in Oriental grocery stores. Medium grain rice may be used if you cannot get the glutinous rice.

(cont'd)

Makes 4-5 servings
Time: 1 hour

Calories: 2056   Carbohydrates: 166 gm
Protein: 95 gm   Fat: 98 gm

(Calculated with ground pork butt)

甜酸肉丸   **SWEET AND SOUR MEAT BALLS**
(Tian Suan Rou Wan)

Ingredients:

        1 lb ground pork or beef
        3 T soy sauce
        1 T sherry
        ¼ t pepper
        1/8 t MSG (optional)
        ½ t onion or garlic powder
        2 T cornstarch
        1 t minced ginger root
        ¼ t salt
           Oil for deep-frying

Method:

1. Mix pork with the next eight ingredients. Form meat into 1" balls.
2. Heat oil to 375-400°. Fry meat balls until brown and done. Set aside. Serve with sauce.   (*cont'd*)

Sweet and Sour sauce:

¼ C catsup
1 T cornstarch
¼ C sugar
2 T vinegar
1 C crushed pineapple
2 t soy sauce
¼ C water
¼ green pepper, cut into bite-size pieces

Put all the ingredients, except green pepper, in a sauce pan. Bring to a boil, stirring constantly. Add meat balls and green pepper; mix well. Serve hot.

One half to one teaspoon of sesame oil can be added before serving.

Fried meat balls can be prepared in advance. Reheat in a preheated 275° oven until hot.

Makes 6 servings
Time: 35 minutes

Calories: 1956   Carbohydrates: 139 gm
Protein: 77 gm   Fat: 118 gm

(Calculated with ground pork butt and 2 T oil for deep-frying)

雪豆炒肝片

LIVER WITH SNOW PEA PODS
(Xue Dou Chao Gan Pian)

Ingredients:

- ½ lb liver (chicken, pork or beef) about 1 cup
- 1½ T soy sauce
- 1 t sherry
- ¼ t pepper
- 1/8 t garlic powder
- 2 t cornstarch
- ¼ lb snow pea pods
- ¾ C bamboo shoots or water chestnuts, sliced
- 2 cloves of garlic, crushed
- 3 thin slices of ginger root
- ¾ C water
- 1 t soy sauce
- 1 chicken bouillon cube
- 2 t cornstarch blended with 2 T of water
- 1 medium size tomato, cut into wedges (optional)
- 4 T oil
- Salt and pepper to taste

Method:

1. Discard all the membranes of the liver and cut into slices (the size of snow pea pods).

2. Mix the liver slices with the next five ingredients.

3. Wash and remove the stems and strings from both ends of the snow pea pods. Cut bamboo shoots or water chestnuts into slices. Set aside.

4. Soften the bouillon cube in ¾ C water.

5. Heat 3 T oil in a teflon pan; sauté crushed garlic and ginger root slices. Add liver and stir-fry until color turns. (Separate liver slices as they cook). Remove to a dish.   (*cont'd*)

72

6. Add 1 T oil. Put in bamboo shoots, snow pea pods, and 1 t soy sauce; stir and mix for 2 minutes.

7. Add dissolved bouillon cube and blended cornstarch. Salt and pepper to taste. Bring to a boil.

8. Add cooked liver and tomato wedges; mix well. Serve hot.

One half to one teaspoon of sesame oil can be added before serving.

Steps 1 and 2 can be prepared in advance.

Makes 6-8 servings
Time: 25 minutes

Calories: 976   Carbohydrates: 37 gm
Protein: 52 gm   Fat: 66 gm

(Calculated with beef liver)

MEAT AND
SOY BEAN SPROUTS
(Dou Ya Chao Rou Si)   豆芽炒肉絲

Ingredients:

     1 lb pork or beef, finely shredded
    ½ lb soy bean sprouts
     6 green onions, finely shredded
     1 t shredded ginger root
     3 T soy sauce
   1/8 t pepper
     4 T oil
        Salt and pepper to taste
     1 T sherry
     1 T cornstarch   (cont'd)

Method:

1. Mix meat with 2 T soy sauce, 1/8 t pepper, 1 T sherry and 1 T cornstarch. Set aside.
2. Clean and wash soy bean sprouts.
3. Heat oil in a teflon pan; add pork. Stir-fry until color turns.
4. Add shredded onions; stir and mix for 1 minute.
5. Add soy bean sprouts and 1 T soy sauce. Stir-fry 5 more minutes (salt and pepper to taste). Serve hot.

One half to one teaspoon of sesame oil can be added before serving.

Makes 6-8 servings
Time: 30 minutes

Calories: 1834   Carbohydrates: 28 gm
Protein: 92 gm   Fat 149 gm

(Calculated with pork)

木樨肉

MOO-SHU PORK OR BEEF
(Mu Xu Rou)

Ingredients:

½   C shredded pork or beef, about ¼ pound
20-25   dried lily buds (golden needles or tiger lily buds)
¼   C dried black wood ears
1   C fresh bean sprouts or 1 C bamboo shoots,
      shredded or 1 C shredded celery
2-3   dried mushrooms, soaked and shredded
3   eggs   *(cont'd)*

¼ t salt
　2　T soy sauce
　1　t cornstarch
　1　t or more shredded ginger root
　1-2　green onions, shredded
　1/8　t MSG (optional)
　½ t sugar
　3　T oil

Method:

1. Soak dried lily buds in hot water for 25 minutes. Drain and knot (see page 212).
2. Soak dried wood ears in hot water for 5-10 minutes. Wash and drain.
3. Mix pork with ½ T soy sauce and 1 t cornstarch.
4. Beat egg with ¼ t salt.
5. Heat 2 T oil in a teflon pan. Scramble eggs and break them into fine pieces. Set aside.
6. Add 1 T oil and stir-fry pork with onions and ginger root for two minutes.
7. Add lily buds, wood ears, bean sprouts, mushrooms, 1½ T soy sauce, 1/8 t MSG and ½ t sugar. Stir and mix for 3 minutes.
8. Add scrambled eggs and mix well.

Serve hot with Chinese pancake (recipe on page 127) or plain rice. Use fingers to serve yourself while eating with Chinese pancakes.

Makes 6 servings
Time: 30 minutes

Calories: 798　　　　　　　　Carbohydrates: 11 gm
Protein: 28 gm　　　　　　　　Fat: 70 gm

(Calculated with pork butt. See page 20).

醃菜炒肉絲

MEAT WITH PICKLED MUSTARD GREENS
(Xian Cai Chao Rou Si)

Ingredients:

                1 lb beef or pork, shredded
                2 T soy sauce
              ¼ t pepper
              ¼ t onion powder
                1 T cornstarch
              ½ C bamboo shoots, shredded
                1 C pickled mustard greens, minced, about ½
                    recipe of mustard greens, (see recipe on page 183)
                1 t sugar
                1 T shredded ginger root
                2 green onions, shredded
            3-4 T oil

Method:

1. Mix meat with the next four ingredients. Set aside.
2. Heat oil in a teflon pan. Add meat; stir-fry until color turns (2-3 minutes). Remove and set aside.
3. Put onions and ginger in remaining oil and sauté for ½ minute. Add mustard greens and bamboo shoots; stir and mix for 2-3 minutes.
4. Add cooked meat and 1 t sugar. Mix well. Serve hot.
The pickled mustard greens should be prepared in advance.

Makes 6 servings
Time: 30 minutes

Calories: 1127   Carbohydrates: 24 gm
Protein: 107 gm   Fat: 65 gm

(Calculated with beef flank steak)

76

PORK WITH CRUSHED GARLIC
(Suan Ni Rou)

蒜泥肉

Ingredients:

    1   lb pork, lean butt, or shoulder
    2   green onions, cut into 1" lengths
    2   slices of ginger root
    1   T sherry
    4   cloves of garlic, finely crushed
    ½   t salt
    2   T soy sauce
    1   t vinegar
    ½   t sugar
    ¼   t pepper
  1-2   T hot sauce (optional)
    1   t sesame oil

Method:

1. Put the first four ingredients in a small sauce pan; cover pork with water. Cover pan and bring to a boil, then lower heat and simmer the pork for 40-50 minutes.

2. Remove the cooked pork to a dish and slice it into ¼" thick pieces. Arrange the pork pieces on a platter.

3. Combine the last eight ingredients in a small bowl and pour over the pork. Serve cold.

Makes 6 servings
Time: 20 minutes

Calories: 1222   Carbohydrates: 9 gm
Protein: 75 gm   Fat: 95 gm

(Calculated with pork butt)

FLUFFY DRIED PORK
(Rou Song)

Ingredients:

    1   lb pork butt, cubed
    1   C water
    1   T oil
    4   T soy sauce
  1½   T sugar
    2   t minced ginger root
   ½   onion, minced
    1   whole star anise
    1   T sherry
   ½   t five-spice powder
  1-2   dried hot peppers, (optional)
   ½   t pepper

Method:

1. Place all the ingredients except oil in a medium sauce pan; cover and bring to a boil.
2. Reduce to low heat and simmer for 1½ hour.
3. Turn to high heat; cook until no juice remains.
4. Heat oil in a non-stick pan. Add cooked pork and stir-fry until the meat dries and becomes fluffy. Break the meat while stir-frying to prevent its burning.

Serve cold.

The fluffy dried pork should melt in your mouth. The Chinese use this pork with hot rice porridge as part of breakfast. It is also very good served as a snack or sprinkled on soup or salad. The meat can be kept for months in a covered jar in the refrigerator.

(cont'd)

Calories: 1382
Protein: 79 gm

Carbohydrates: 24 gm
Fat: 105 gm

**STEAMED BLACK
BEAN SPARERIBS**
(Dou Shi Zheng Pai Gu)

豆豉蒸排骨

Ingredients:

  1 lb spareribs (ask the butcher to chop them into 1" pieces)
  1 T crushed garlic
  1 t minced ginger root
  3 T black beans (about 1 oz), soaked in 1 T water
  1 t soy sauce
  1 t (or more) minced hot peppers (optional)
  1 T cornstarch

Method:

  1. Mash the soaked beans into a paste.
  2. Mix the chopped spareribs with the last six ingredients.
  3. Put the spareribs in a heat-proof dish and place the dish in a tier of a steamer.
  4. Steam over boiling water for 40 minutes (never open the lid of the steamer while steaming). Serve hot.

Makes 4-6 servings
Time: 40 minutes

Calories: 1184
Protein: 43 gm

Carbohydrates: 5 gm
Fat: 106 gm

糖醋排骨

SWEET SOUR SPARERIBS
(Tang Cu Pai Gu)

Ingredients:

  2 lb lean spareribs, (ask the butcher to chop
    them into 1" pieces)
  3 green onions, shredded
  3 slices of ginger root
  5 T soy sauce
  1 T sherry
1/8 t pepper
  1 T cornstarch
  2 cloves of garlic, crushed
  1 C oil for deep-frying
  5 T brown sugar
  1 T cornstarch
  3 T vinegar
  ¼ C water
  1 t sesame oil

Method:

1. Mix the spareribs with the next five ingredients and marinate for 30 minutes at room temperature. Turn them several
times for even flavor.

2. Mix the last five ingredients in a small bowl. Set aside.

3. Transfer the marinated spareribs to a bowl; mix them
with 1 T cornstarch. Save the soy sauce and onion for later
use.

4. Heat oil in a pan; deep-fry spareribs until done (no
bloody liquid comes out when cut, about 3-4 minutes.) Remove to a dish.

5. Pour out the deep-fry oil until only 1 T of oil is left in
(cont'd)

80

the pan. Brown the garlic. Add the sauce mixture from step two and soy sauce from step three. Stir and cook until the sauce thickens.

6. Add fried spareribs and mix well. Serve hot.

Makes 6 servings
Time: 40 minutes

Calories: 2467   Carbohydrates: 80 gm
Protein: 84gm   Fat: 199gm

(Calculated with 3 T oil for deep-frying)

BARBECUED SPARERIBS
(Kao Pai Gu)

烤排骨

Ingredients:

    2 lb lean spareribs (ask the butcher to chop them into 1" pieces)
    2 green onions, shredded
    ½ inch ginger root, crushed
    ¼ t pepper
    1 T sherry
    1 T soy sauce
    1 T honey
    2 cloves of garlic, crushed
    5 T Hoisin sauce

Method:

1. In a small bowl, combine all the ingredients except spareribs.

(cont'd)

2. Place the spareribs in a larger bowl and pour the sauce mixture on the spareribs. Stir until they are well mixed. Let them marinate for 2-3 hours at room temperature or keep in refrigerator overnight. Turn thoroughly several times for even flavor.

3. Preheat broiler. Place the spareribs on a rack in a shallow pan, 6" from the broiler. Broil the spareribs for 15 minutes. Turn the spareribs and broil for 15 minutes more. The door of the broiler should be open a little while broiling.

4. Serve hot or cold as they are or with plum sauce.

Makes 6 servings
Time: 40 minutes

Calories: 1810   Carbohydrates: 22 gm
Protein: 80 gm   153 gm

(See page 20)

红烧蹄膀

**BRAISED PORK HOCK
OR PORK SHOULDER**
(Hung Shao Ti Pang)

Ingredients:

    2-4 lb pork hock or pork shoulder
     ½   C soy sauce
     3   whole star anise
     1   onion, chopped
     4   thin slices of ginger root
     1   small stick of cinnamon
     1   T sherry
     4   T brown sugar
         Water

(cont'd)

Method:

1. Place meat in a sauce pan and add all the ingredients except the water and the sugar.
2. Fill the pan with water (about ½" above the meat).
3. Bring to a boil and continue boiling for 10 minutes.
4. Reduce to low heat and simmer for 2 hours in the covered pan. Let cool.
5. Keep the meat in the refrigerator in the same pan overnight.
6. Discard all the hardened fat. Cook over medium heat until about ¾ C of water is left. Add the sugar and cook another 5 minutes.

Serve hot with plain rice or Chinese bread.

This dish needs no special attention while cooking. The leftovers can be reheated and served. It is also good cooked with string beans, Chinese cabbage, turnips (cubed) or spinach.

The meat can be prepared in advance and kept in the refrigerator for days or in the freezer for weeks without any harm. Reheat before serving.

One ounce of dried cabbage (Cai Gan 菜乾, 霉乾菜) can be added before the sauce evaporates.

Makes 6-8 servings
Time: 2¼ hours

Calories: 4399   Carbohydrates: 74 gm
Protein: 258 gm   Fat: 338 gm

(Calculated with 4 pounds of pork shoulder with bone and skin.)

白切肉

WHITE CUT MEAT
(Bai Qie Rou)

Ingredients:

2-3 lb pork, (any cut)
3-4 T soy sauce (Mushroom soy sauce is preferred.
This sauce has been recently imported from
mainland China.)
1-2 t sesame oil

Method:

1. Place pork in a deep sauce pan. Add enough water to cover the pork. Cover pan and bring to a boil.
2. Reduce to medium heat and cook for one hour.
3. Remove pork to a dish and cool to room temperature.
4. Slice pork into ¼" thick pieces; arrange neatly on a plate.
5. Mix soy sauce and sesame oil together; pour on meat before serving or dip the pork in the sauce mixture before eating.

This dish does not require constant attention while cooking.

Makes 6-8 servings
Time: 70 minutes

Calories: 2350
Protein: 152 gm

Carbohydrates: 4 gm
Fat: 186 gm

(Calculated with 2 pounds of pork butt)

STIR-FRY PORKLOIN
WITH GREEN ONION
(Cong Bao Li Ji)

蔥爆里肌

Ingredients:

    1 lb pork tenderloin
    2 T soy sauce
    1 t sherry
  ¼ t pepper
    4 cloves of garlic, finely crushed
    1 T cornstarch
    3 T oil
6-7 green onions, cut into 1" sections
    2 T soy sauce
    1 t brown sugar
    1 t sesame oil

Method:

1. Cut the pork into 2" x 1" x 1/6" slices. Mix the pork with the next five ingredients.

2. Heat oil in a non-stick pan; stir-fry pork until color turns (5 minutes).

3. Add the last four ingredients; stir-fry until the green onions are cooked. Serve hot.

Makes 6 servings
Time: 15 minutes

Calories: 1388   Carbohydrates: 13 gm
Protein: 96 gm   Fat: 98 gm

义烧肉

Ingredients:

> 2 lb pork butt or pork loin, cut into 1½" wide x
>   1" thick strips
> ¼ t pepper
> 2 T soy sauce
> 2 green onions, cut into 2" long pieces
> 4 thin slices of ginger root
> 1 T sherry
> ⅓ C Hoisin Sauce

Method:

1. Mix all the ingredients together. Set aside and let stand at room temperature for 2 hours or keep in refrigerator overnight. Turn occasionally for even flavor.

2. Preheat broiler. Place the pork strips on a rack in a shallow pan, 6" away from the broiler. Broil the pork for 10 minutes, turn and broil for 10 minutes more. The door of the oven should be slightly open while broiling.

3. Cut into slices. Serve hot or cold.

Sliced pork can be used as a filling for broiled pork stuffed buns. It also can be used for fried rice (recipes on pages 277 and 226).

Broiled pork can be kept in the refrigerator for a few days or in the freezer for weeks. Reheat the meat in the oven before serving. This pork may be served as a main dish, appetizer, side dish or sandwich meat.

Makes 6 servings
Time: 25 minutes

Calories: 2316   Carbohydrates: 5 gm
Protein: 152 gm   Fat: 182 gm

(Calculated with pork butt. See page 20)

SWEET AND SOUR PORK
(Gu Lao Rou)

Ingredients:

    1 lb pork (butt, shoulder, loin, etc.), cut into cubes the size of canned pineapple chunks
    3 T soy sauce
    1 T sherry
    ¼ t pepper
    ¼ t onion or garlic powder
    1 small egg
  1/8 t MSG (optional)
  4-6 T cornstarch
    2 C vegetable oil for deep-frying

Method:

1. Mix pork with the next six ingredients.
2. Add 4 T cornstarch to pork and mix well. If the coating is too drippy, add more cornstarch.
3. Heat oil to 375-400° in a medium sauce pan or in a wok. Carefully drop the pork pieces into the hot oil one by one. Fry until golden brown.
4. Keep the fried pork in a heated oven while preparing the sauce (*next page*). Serve with sauce.

One half to one teaspoon of sesame oil can be added before serving.

(*cont'd*)

SWEET AND SOUR SAUCE

¼ C catsup
2 T cornstarch
½ C sugar
¼ C vinegar
1 C pineapple syrup (from the can)
1 C canned pineapple tidbits or pineapple chunks
1 T soy sauce
½ green pepper, cut into bite-size pieces

Put all the ingredients, except the green pepper, in a small sauce pan; mix well. Bring the sauce to a boil, stirring constantly while it cooks. Add green pepper; pour sauce over the cooked pork before serving.

Steps 1 and 2 of the "Method" can be prepared in advance.

The fried pork can be refrigerated or frozen. Before serving, reheat the pork pieces in a 300° oven until hot.

Makes 6 servings
Time: 40 minutes

Calories: 2729
Protein: 85 gm

Carbohydrates: 251 gm
Fat: 152 gm

(Calculated with pork butt and 4 T oil for deep-frying.)

PORK AND SHIRMP CHOP SUEY
(Chao Shi Sui)

炒什碎

Ingredients:

- ½ lb pork, diced
- ¼ lb shelled shrimp, fresh or frozen
- 2-4 oz fresh mushrooms, diced
- 1 C frozen peas and carrots (about ½ oz)
- ½ C diced celery
- ½ C water chestnuts, sliced
- ½ green pepper, diced
- ½ onion, diced
- 4 T soy sauce
- 2 t sherry
- ¼ t pepper
- 2 t cornstarch
- 1/8 t MSG (optional)
- 4 T oil

Method:

1. Mix pork with 2 T soy sauce, 1 t sherry, 1/8 t pepper and 1 t cornstarch. Set aside.
2. Mix shrimp with ¼ t salt, 1 t sherry, 1/8 t pepper and 1 t cornstarch. Set aside.
3. Heat 2 T oil in a teflon pan; add pork. Stir-fry until color turns. Remove to a dish. Add 1 T oil and shrimp. Stir-fry for 2 minutes. Remove the shrimp to a dish.
4. Add 1 T oil; sauté onion. Add mushrooms, celery, water chestnuts, green pepper, 1 T soy sauce, peas and carrots and salt and pepper to taste. Stir and mix for 2 minutes.
5. Add cooked pork and shrimp; stir and mix for 1 minute. Serve hot.

(cont'd)

One half to one teaspoon of sesame oil can be added before serving.

Makes 6 servings
Time: 20 minutes

Calories: 1239
Protein: 76 gm

Carbohydrates: 41 gm
Fat: 84 gm

(Calculated with pork loin)

HOISIN SAUCE PORK
(Tian Jiang Rou Si)

Ingredients:

- ½ lb shredded pork butt
- 2 t sherry
- ¼ t pepper
- ¼ t garlic powder
- 1 t soy sauce
- 1 t cornstarch
- 4 T oil
- 3 green onions, shredded
- 1 t shredded ginger root
- 3 T Hoisin sauce
- ½ C shredded carrots
- ½ C diced water chestnuts
- ½ C shredded bamboo shoots
- 2 C shredded celery cabbage

(cont'd)

Method:

1. Mix pork with the next five ingredients.
2. Heat oil in a non-stick pan. Add pork and stir-fry for 5 minutes. Separate pork shreds while stir-frying.
3. Add onion and ginger root; stir-fry for 1 minute.
4. Add Hoisin sauce. Stir and mix thoroughly.
5. Add carrots, water chestnuts, bamboo shoots and celery cabbage. Stir and cook for 5 minutes more. Serve hot with rice.

Makes 4-6 servings
Time: 20 minutes

Calories: 1126   Carbohydrates: 9 gm
Protein: 40 gm   Fat: 102 gm

(See page 20)

回鍋肉

DOUBLE COOKED PORK
(Hui Guo Rou)

Ingredients:

- 1 lb pork, butt or shoulder
- 1 leek, washed and cut into 1" long strips (about ¼ lb)
- 1 medium red sweet pepper, diced
- 3 small hot peppers, shredded
- 2 T soy sauce
- 3 T Hoisin sauce
- ½ t pepper
- 1 T sherry
- 3 slices of ginger root

Method:

1. Put the pork in a sauce pan; add 2 C water and cook for 20 minutes. Let the cooked pork cool in a dish. Slice the cold, cooked pork into 1/8" slices.

2. Heat oil in a pan; add pork slices and Hoisin sauce. Stir-fry for 5 minutes.

3. Add leek, soy sauce, ginger and hot pepper. Stir-fry for 3 minutes.

4. Add sweet pepper, sherry and pepper. Stir-fry for 3 more minutes. Serve hot.

Makes 6 servings
Time: 30 minutes

Calories: 1216   Carbohydrates: 14 gm
Protein: 77 gm   Fat: 91 gm

(Calculated with pork butt. See page 20).

LION'S HEAD (LARGE MEAT BALLS)
(Si Zi Tou)

獅子頭

Ingredients:

- 3 lb ground pork
- 4 T soy sauce
- 1 t salt
- ¼ t pepper
- 1 T minced ginger root
- 2 green onions, minced
- 1 T sherry
- 1/8 t MSG (optional)
- 3-4 dried mushrooms, soaked and minced (optional)
- 2 T cornstarch
- 1½ C water
- ½ C oil
- 1 lb celery cabbage (Chinese cabbage), cut into 2" lengths
- 1 green onion, cut into 1" pieces
- 3 thin slices of ginger root
- 1 T soy sauce, or to taste
- 1 t brown sugar

Method:

1. Mix the first eight ingredients (also mushrooms, if desired) together well. Add cornstarch; mix well. Divide the meat into 5 to 6 meat balls.

2. Heat oil; brown meat balls.

3. Pour off oil. Add 1½ C water, green onions, ginger root and 1 T soy sauce; cover pan and bring to a boil.

4. Reduce to low heat and simmer for 1 hour.

5. Add celery cabbage, 1 t brown sugar and cook over medium heat until ¼ C of water is left. Serve hot.   (cont'd)

This dish does not require constant attention while cooking. Cooked meat balls can be refrigerated or frozen before adding vegetables.

Makes 8-10 servings
Time: 1¼ hours

Calories: 3672

Carbohydrates: 29 gm

Protein: 228 gm

Fat: 283 gm

(Calculated with ground pork butt and 1 T oil for browning.)

poultry

FRIED SPICED CHICKEN
(Zha Ji)

Ingredients:

1 frying chicken, 2-3 pounds
2 cloves of garlic, crushed
3 T soy sauce
1/8 t pepper
1 t sherry
1 egg
4-6 T cornstarch
Oil for deep-frying

Method:

1. Cut the chicken into halves, then cut the halves into small pieces (1½").
2. Mix the cut-up chicken with the next five ingredients. Add 4T cornstarch first; if the batter is too drippy then add more cornstarch.
3. Heat oil to 375-400°. Gently drop chicken pieces one by one into the hot oil. Fry until golden brown. Serve hot or cold.

Steps 1 and 2 of the "Method" can be prepared in advance. Fried chicken can be reheated in the oven.

Makes 8-10 servings
Time: 20 minutes

Calories: 1244   Carbohydrates: 31 gm
Protein: 123 gm   Fat: 64 gm

(Calculated with 2 pounds of chicken 2 T of oil for deep-frying)

BLACK BEAN CHICKEN
(Dou Shi Ji)

Ingredients:

 1 chicken (about two pounds), cut into bite size
   pieces
 2 cloves of garlic, crushed
 4 thin slices of ginger root
 1 t sherry
 3 T black beans (about 1 oz) soaked in 1 T water
 3 T soy sauce
 1 t brown sugar
 1 T oil

Method:

1. Mash soaked beans into a paste.
2. Heat oil in a deep sauce pan. Sauté garlic, ginger and bean paste for ½ minute.
3. Add chicken, 1 t sherry, 3 T soy sauce and 1 t brown sugar. Stir and cook for 5 minutes.
4. Add ½ C water. Cover pan and cook until ¼ C water remains. Serve hot.

This is a very tasty and easy-to-make dish. The black beans can be purchased from an Oriental grocery store in one half or one pound cans or in plastic bags. They are highly seasoned and very salty. Transfer the black beans into a jar after the package (or can) is opened. Black beans can be stored for a long time in a covered jar.

Makes 6-8 servings
Time: 20 minutes

(cont'd)

Calories: 982   Carbohydrates: 11 gm
Protein: 122 gm   Fat: 46 gm

(Calculated with 2 pounds of ready to cook fryers.)

加厘雞

CHICKEN WITH CURRY
(Ka Li Ji)

Ingredients:

    1 chicken, about 2-3 pounds
  2-3 T curry powder, mixed with 2 T water
    2 medium size potatoes, peeled and cubed
    1 onion, diced
    3 T soy sauce
   ½ t salt
   ½ t pepper
   ½ C water
    1 T oil

Method:

1. Cut chicken into 1½" chunks. Mix curry powder with water.

2. Have the cubed potatoes and diced onion ready.

3. Heat oil in a deep sauce pan; brown onion. Add chicken, curry paste, soy sauce, salt and pepper; stir and mix for 5 minutes.

4. Add potato cubes; stir and mix for 2 minutes.

5. Add ½ C water. Bring to a boil.

6. Cover pan. Turn to medium heat and cook for 20 minutes. If it is too dry, add a little water. Serve hot.   (*cont'd*)

If you like "hot" food, add two or more dried hot peppers (chili) while browning the chicken.

Dried hot peppers can be purchased from regular supermarkets or Oriental grocery stores. They are dark red in color.

Makes 6 servings
Time: 30 minutes

Calories: 1118	Carbohydrates: 50 gm
Protein: 121 gm	Fat: 44 gm

(See page 20)

WHITE CUT CHICKEN
(Bai Qie Ji)

佝切雞

Ingredients:

- 1 chicken, about 2 pounds, cut into two halves
- 3 thin slices of ginger root
- 1 T sherry
- 2 green onions, cut into halves
- ⅓ C soy sauce (mushroom soy sauce is preferable to regular soy sauce)
- 1 T sesame oil

Method:

1. Using a large deep sauce pan, add enough water to cover the chicken. (Chicken will be put in the water later.)
2. Boil water with ginger, sherry and onion.
3. Submerge chicken into the boiling water. Cover pan and bring to a boil again. *(cont'd)*

4. Turn off the heat. Keep the chicken in the hot water and covered pan for 6 hours. Do not open the cover during the waiting period.

5. Place the cooked chicken in the refrigerator until chilled.

6. Cut the chicken into bite-size pieces; arrange them on a large platter. Brush sesame oil on the chicken pieces.

7. Dip the chicken pieces in soy sauce before eating or pour soy sauce on the chicken pieces before serving. Serve cold.

Thanks goes to my good friend Mrs. Wong, who so kindly told me the secret of making this tender, juicy chicken.

Since this dish is served cold, it must be prepared in advance.

When cutting the chicken, cut through the joints first, then chop into smaller pieces. If you find the chopping job too difficult, carve the chicken as you would a roasted chicken.

Makes 8-10 servings

Calories: 944   Carbohydrates: 8 gm
Protein: 119 gm   Fat: 44 gm

油淋雞

OIL DRIPPING CHICKEN
(You Lin Ji)

Ingredients:

1 fryer, about 2 pounds
4 T minced green onion
2 T minced ginger root
2 t salt
3 T oil
1 T sherry
Water

(cont'd)

Method:

1. Mix minced onion, ginger root and salt together. Set aside.

2. Place chicken in a deep sauce pan. Add water until the chicken is half covered. Add sherry.

3. Boil the chicken for 15 minutes; turn to other side and boil for 15 minutes more.

4. Cut the chicken into bite sizes; arrange them on a platter.

5. Heat oil in a small sauce pan until very hot. Reduce heat; add onion mixture and stir for ½ minute.

6. Pour the oil mixture on chicken pieces until all the pieces are bathed with the flavored oil. Serve hot or cold.

You may save the water to make a home made chicken broth.

One half to one teaspoon of sesame oil can be added before serving.

Makes 6-8 servings
Time: 35 minutes

Calories: 1161   Carbohydrates: 3 gm
Protein: 115 gm   Fat: 72 gm

鹽水雞

Ingredients:

      3 t salt
      ¼ t MSG (optional)
      ½ t white pepper
      ½ t ginger powder
      ½ t onion powder
      ½ t ground thyme
      1 fryer, about 2 pounds

Method:

1. Mix the first six ingredients together. Rub the mixture evenly on the chicken. Put the chicken in a large plastic bag and keep in the refrigerator overnight.

2. Use a large sauce pan. Fill the pan with enough water to cover the chicken (the chicken will be put in the pan after the water boils).

3. Bring the water to a boil and submerge the chicken in the boiling water. Cover pan and bring to a boil; continue boiling for 1 minute.

4. Turn off the heat. Let the chicken stay in the hot water for six hours. Do not open the lid during the waiting period.

5. Chill the chicken in the refrigerator for a few hours.

6. Cut the chicken into big pieces. Serve cold.

You may use the chicken as a lunch or for a picnic.

Makes 8-10 servings

Calories: 764
Protein: 115 gm

Carbohydrates: trace
Fat: 30 gm

CHICKEN WITH CHESTNUTS
(Li Zi Ji)

Ingredients:

    1 chicken, about 2 pounds
    ¾ C dried chestnuts (about ¼ pound) or 200 gm
        fresh chestnuts
    1 T oil
    2 cloves of garlic, crushed
    5 T soy sauce
    3 green onions, shredded
    3 slices of ginger root
    1 T sherry
    1 T brown sugar
    ¼ C water

Method:

1. Cut chicken into 2" square pieces.
2. Soak the dried chestnuts in hot water for 1 hour; clean the skin. If fresh chestnuts are used, just remove the shell and skin.
3. Heat oil in a deep sauce pan; brown garlic. Add chicken and the last six ingredients; stir and mix for 2 minutes.
4. Cover pan and simmer the chicken for 10 minutes.
5. Add chestnuts and cook over high heat for 10 minutes. Serve hot.

Makes 6-8 servings
Time: 30 minutes

Calories: 1431   Carbohydrates: 111 gm
Protein: 127 gm   Fat: 49 gm

Ingredients:

   3 t salt
  ½ t white pepper
  ¼ t onion powder
  ¼ t ground thyme
  1 C, or more, dry sherry
  1 fryer, about 2 pounds

Method:

1. Quarter the chicken.
2. Mix the first five ingredients and rub the mixture on the chicken pieces.
3. Put the chicken in a bowl and put the bowl in a boiling steamer. Steam over high heat for 30 minutes.
4. Remove the steamed chicken into a deep bowl.
5. Pour the sherry mixture over the steamed chicken. Cover and keep the chicken in the refrigerator for 24 hours. Turn the pieces once or twice during the waiting period.
6. Cut into bite size pieces and serve cold.

Makes 6-8 servings

Calories: 957
Protein: 115 gm

Carbohydrates: 10 gm
Fat: 30 gm

MUSHROOM CHICKEN
(Dong Ku Ji)

Ingredients:

    1 small chicken, 2-3 pounds
   10 dried mushrooms
 2-3 cloves of garlic
 2-3 slices of ginger root
    1 T sherry
    4 T soy sauce
  ½ C water
      Salt and pepper to taste

Method:

1. Cut chicken into bite-size (1½" x 1½") pieces. Crush garlic.

2. Soak mushrooms in hot water for 20 minutes. Squeeze them dry and cut into quarters.

3. Put all the ingredients in a medium sauce pan; cover and bring to a boil.

4. Cook for 10 minutes at medium heat or until only a few tablespoons of water remain. Turn several times while cooking.

Makes 6-8 servings
Time: 35 minutes

Calories: 850   Carbohydrates: 10 gm
Protein: 118 gm   Fat: 31 gm.

(Calculated with 2 pounds of chicken)

大千雞

TA-CHAN CHICKEN
(Ta Qian Ji)

Ingredients:

1 small chicken or half a large chicken, about 2
  pounds
2 (or more) red dried hot peppers, cut into
  ½" pieces
4 cloves of garlic, crushed
4 thin slices of ginger root
1 T sherry
4 T soy sauce
1 T oil
1 t brown sugar

Method:

1. Cut chicken into bite-size pieces.
2. Heat oil in a pan. Brown the garlic, ginger and hot
pepper.
3. Add the chicken, 3 T soy sauce, 1 T sherry, and brown
sugar; stir and cook for 5 minutes.
4. Reduce to medium heat. Cover and cook for 8-10 minutes. If it is too dry, add a little water. Serve hot.

I learned this dish from the owner of a well known Chinese
restaurant in Brasil. He used to be the cook for the famous
Chinese artist, Mr. Ta-Chan Chiang. This dish is Mr. Chiang's
favorite. Mr. Chiang was from Szechwan where highly spiced
and hot dishes are favored.

Makes 6 servings
Time: 25 minutes

Calories: 936   Carbohydrates: 7 gm
Protein: 117 gm   Fat: 44 gm

106

SMOKED CHICKEN
(Xun Ji)

Ingredients:

    1   chicken, about 2 pounds
    1   T Szechwan brown peppercorns (Hua Chiao)
    1   T salt
    1   green onion, or more
    4   thin slices of ginger root
    2   whole star anise
    1   cinnamon stick, or more
    1   C soy sauce
    ½   C sugar
    ½   C flour
    ½   C black tea leaves
        Water
        Sesame oil

Method:

1. Roast peppercorns at medium heat in a small sauce pan on top of stove for 2 minutes. Shake pan constantly to prevent burning. Add 1 T salt and roast 2 more minutes in the same manner.

2. Roll, crush or blend in a covered blender the roasted peppercorns into a fine powder.

3. Rub the peppercorn powder on the chicken inside and out. Wrap it in a plastic bag and keep it in the refrigerator for 6 hours or overnight.

4. Fill a large deep sauce pan ⅓ full of water. Add onion, ginger, star anise, cinnamon and soy sauce; cover and bring to a boil. Turn to medium heat and cook for 10 minutes.

5. Add chicken to the boiling sauce; cover and cook for 10 minutes. Turn chicken and cook for 10 minutes more.

6. Remove chicken; let cool to room temperature.

7. Place a layer of foil on the bottom of a large deep sauce pan. Spread sugar, flour and tea leaves on the foil. Put a rack over the tea leaves and place the chicken on the rack.

8. Cover pan and smoke over low heat for 10 minutes. Turn the chicken to the other side and smoke for 5-8 minutes more. Do not open the lid while chicken is smoking.

9. Remove chicken from pan, brush with sesame oil. Cut into bite size pieces. Serve cold.

The sauce from step 5 of the "Method" can be reused for the same purpose. Step 7 of the "Method" can be used to smoke 2 or 3 chickens, one after another. Smoked chicken can be frozen.

Pine needles can be added along with the tea leaves in step 7 to add a delicate pine flavor.

Calories: 764　　　　　　　Carbohydrates: trace
Protein: 115 gm　　　　　　Fat: 30 gm

CHICKEN FOO YOUNG
(Fu Rong Ji)

Ingredients:

　½　lb chicken breast, boned and diced
　4　egg whites
1/8　t onion powder
　1　t sherry
　½　t salt
　½　C chicken broth (canned)

(cont'd)

```
1/8  t white pepper
1/8  t MSG (optional)
  1  T cornstarch
  4  T oil
  1  T egg shreds, minced (recipe on page 242)
  2  T minced ham (about 1 ounce)
10-15  fresh snow pea pods, washed and with the ends
       snapped off or ½ C frozen peas, thawed
  1  C chicken broth
  1  T cornstarch blended with 1 T water
```

Method:

1. Blend the first eight ingredients in a blender until the mixture becomes a smooth paste.

2. Remove the paste to a bowl. Mix with 1 T cornstarch.

3. Heat oil in a teflon pan over low heat.

4. Drop 1 heaping teaspoonful of the paste into the oil. When the paste turns white and firm, turn and cook for a few seconds. Remove to a dish. Repeat until the paste is used up. The cooked paste should be white in color, not brown!

5. Add chicken broth and blended cornstarch in the same pan. Stir and cook until the liquid thickens.

6. Fold in snow pea pods first, then fold in cooked chicken very gently and bring to a boil. Remove to a serving dish, garnish with minced ham and minced egg shreds. Serve hot.

One half to one teaspoon of sesame oil can be added before serving.

Makes 6-8 servings
Time: 40 minutes

Calories: 952   Carbohydrates: 21 gm
Protein: 54 gm   Fat: 68 gm

蘇姑雞片

Ingredients:

- ½ lb chicken breast, sliced (1" x 1½" x 1/6")
- ½ t onion powder
- 2 ginger root slices
- ¼ t pepper
- ½ t salt
- 1 t sherry
- 1/8 t MSG
- 1 t cornstarch
- ¼ lb fresh mushrooms, sliced
- 1 small green pepper, diced
- 2 T soy sauce
- ¼ C water
- 1 t cornstarch blended with 1 T water
- 4 T oil
- 1 onion, minced

Method:

1. Mix the chicken slices with the next seven ingredients.

2. Heat oil in a non-stick pan; brown onion. Add chicken and stir constantly until the color of the chicken meat turns whitish (about 2 minutes). Remove to a dish.

3. Put the mushrooms, green pepper, soy sauce, water and blended cornstarch in the pan and bring to a boil.

4. Add the cooked chicken slices to the vegetables and stir for 1 minute. Serve immediately.

One half to one teaspoon of sesame oil can be added before serving.

Makes 4-6 servings

(cont'd)

Time: 25 minutes

Calories: 820   Carbohydrates: 26 gm
Protein: 34 gm   Fat: 64 gm

CHICKEN AND NUTS
(Chao Ji Ding)

Ingredients:

    1 t sherry
    ¼ t onion powder
    1/8 t pepper
    2 T cornstarch
    2 thin slices of ginger root
    1/8 t MSG (optional)
    1 lb chicken breast, diced
    4 T soy sauce
    ½ small onion, chopped or 2 cloves of garlic,
      crushed
    1 C diced celery
    ½ C water chestnuts, diced or ½ C bamboo shoots,
      diced
    1 C diced green pepper (red ones are preferable
      to green ones)
    1 t cornstarch blended with 1 T water
    ½ C water
    ¼ C walnuts, cashews, peanuts or almonds (you
      could use more)
    4 T oil
      Pinch of pepper and MSG to taste.   *(cont'd)*

Method:

1. Use 3 T soy sauce to marinate chicken with first six ingredients.

2. Heat oil in a teflon pan; stir-fry nuts until light brown (takes less than 1 minute). Remove fried nuts to a small bowl.

3. Stir-fry chicken in the remaining oil until color turns; remove to a dish.

4. Sauté onion or garlic in the remaining oil. Add celery, pepper, water chestnuts, 1 T soy sauce, ½ C water, 1 t blended cornstarch, pinch of pepper and MSG to taste. Stir and mix for 1 minute.

5. Mix with cooked chicken. Remove to a serving dish and garnish with fried nuts. Serve hot.

One half to one teaspoon of sesame oil can be added before serving.

Step 1 of the "Method" can be prepared in advance. The marinated chicken can be frozen for weeks. Before using, thaw completely. When you have time, I suggest you do the first step ahead of time. You will have less work and pressure while cooking this dish and will enjoy it more.

Makes 6-8 servings
Time: 35 minutes

Calories: 1275
Protein: 86 gm

Carbohydrates: 46 gm
Fat: 84 gm

CHICKEN BREAST WITH BLACK WALNUTS
(Hu Tao Ji Pu)

胡桃雞脯

Ingredients:

- 1 lb chicken breast
- ½ C black walnuts
- 5 T oil
- 3 T soy sauce
- 1 egg white
- 2 t sherry
- ¼ t onion powder
- ¼ t pepper
- 1 T cornstarch

Method:

1. Cut the chicken breast into 4 pieces. Pound the chicken into ½" thick fillets.

2. Mix the last six ingredients in a small bowl; pour on the chicken breast. Marinate the chicken for 30 minutes. Stir occasionally for even flavor.

3. Chop the black walnuts into fine pieces. Coat the chicken fillets with a thin layer of chopped walnuts.

4. Heat oil and add walnut-coated chicken fillets. Fry over medium heat until golden brown (about 1½ minutes). Serve hot as it is, with your favorite sauce or with Hua Chiao powder (see page 122, step 2).

Makes 4 servings
Time: 40 minutes

Calories: 1496
Protein: 94 gm

Carbohydrates: 20 gm
Fat: 116 gm

醬爆雞丁

**CHICKEN BREAST
WITH HOISIN SAUCE**
(Jiang Bao Ji Ding)

Ingredients:

- ¾ lb chicken breast, cubed (½" x ½" x ½")
- 1 T soy sauce
- 1 t sherry
- ½ t pepper
- 2 ginger root slices
- ½ t onion powder
- 2 t cornstarch
- ½ C water chestnuts (about 3 oz), diced
- 1 green pepper, diced
- 3-4 dried mushrooms, soaked and diced
- ½ C bamboo shoots, diced
- 3 T Hoisin sauce
- 4 T oil
- 2 green onions, minced

Method:

1. Mix the chicken with the next six ingredients.
2. Heat oil in a non-stick pan; brown onion. Add chicken and stir for 2 minutes.
3. Add water chestnuts, green pepper, mushrooms, bamboo shoots, and Hoisin sauce to the chicken; stir for 5-7 minutes. Serve immediately.

Makes 6 servings
Time: 20 minutes

Calories: 917
Protein: 60 gm

Carbohydrates: 27 gm
Fat: 63 gm

(See page 20)

SOY SAUCE CHICKEN
(Jiang You Ji)

醬 油 雞

Ingredients:

   1 lb drum sticks
   1 lb thighs
   ½ C soy sauce
   1-2 whole star anise
   1 stick of cinnamon
   ¼ t thyme
   4 thin slices of ginger root
   1 T sherry
   1 T brown sugar
   1 T honey

Method:

   1. Marinate the drum sticks and thighs with the next eight ingredients for 2 hours or more, stirring occasionally.
   2. Cook and stir the chicken over medium heat in a deep sauce pan until the soy sauce and the juice from the chicken are almost dried.
   3. Add 1 C water, cover pan and cook for 8-10 minutes over high heat or until all the water is evaporated. Serve hot or cold.

Makes 6 servings
Time 15-20 minutes

Calories: 940
Protein: 120 gm

Carbohydrates: 39 gm
Fat: 30 gm

杏仁雞丁

CHICKEN WITH ALMONDS
(Xing Ren Ji Ding)

Ingredients:

- 1 lb chicken breast, diced
- 1 T soy sauce
- ¼ t onion powder
- ¼ t pepper
- 2 slices of ginger root
- 1 T sherry
- 2 t cornstarch
- ½ C roasted almonds
- 4 T oil
- 1 sweet pepper (red color is preferred), diced
- ½ C water chestnuts, diced
- 4 black mushrooms, soaked and diced
- 2 green onions, minced
- 4 T Hoisin sauce

Method:

1. Mix chicken with the next six ingredients.
2. Heat 3 T oil in a non-stick pan; add chicken and stir-fry until color turns (2 minutes). Remove to a dish.
3. Add 1 T oil and the last five ingredients; stir and mix for 2 minutes.
4. Add cooked chicken and mix well.
5. Add almonds. Mix and serve.

Makes 6 servings
Time: 25 minutes

Calories: 1416   Carbohydrates: 33 gm
Protein: 90 gm   Fat: 103 gm   (*cont'd*)

(See page 20)

SAUTEED CHICKEN WINGS
(Cong Lin Ji Chi)

Ingredients:

    2   lb chicken wings (cut through joints and discard tips)
    4   slices of ginger root
    6   T soy sauce
    1   T sherry
  1/8   t pepper
    1   t sugar
    1   T oil
  3-6   green onions, minced

Method:

1. Heat 1 T oil over medium heat in a sauce pan. Add chicken wings, ginger root, soy sauce and pepper; stir and cook for 8 minutes.

2. Add sherry and sugar. Stir and cook for 1 minute.

3. Add minced onion; stir and cook for 2 minutes. Serve hot or cold.

One half to one teaspoon of sesame oil can be added before serving.

Makes 6-8 servings
Time: 15 minutes

Calories: 855   Carbohydrates: 14 gm
Protein: 86 gm   Fat: 47 gm

BARBECUED CHICKEN WINGS
(Kao Ji Chi)

Ingredients:

- 2 lb chicken wings (cut through joints and discard tips)
- 2 green onions, shredded
- 5 slices of ginger root
- ¼ t pepper
- 1 T sherry
- 1 T soy sauce
- 1 T honey
- 2 cloves of garlic, crushed
- 5 T Hoisin sauce

Method:

1. Combine all the ingredients, except chicken wings, in a small bowl.

2. Place the chicken in a large bowl, pour the sauce mixture on the chicken wings and let them marinate in the sauce for 2-3 hours. Turn the chicken several times for even flavor.

3. Pre-heat broiler. Place the chicken wings on a rack in a shallow pan, 6" from the broiler. Broil the chicken wings for 15 minutes. Turn them over and broil for 15 minutes more. The door of the broiler should be open slightly while broiling.

4. Serve hot or cold.

Makes 6 servings
Time: 40 minutes

Calories: 748   Carbohydrates: 21 gm
Protein: 82 gm   Fat: 33 gm

(See page 20)

BEAN SPROUTS
AND CHICKEN SALAD
(Ji Si Ban Dou Ya)

雞絲拌豆芽

Ingredients:

    1 lb fresh bean sprouts, mung bean or soy beans
    ½ lb chicken breast
    1 C shredded celery hearts
    1 green onion, finely shredded
    1 t finely shredded ginger root
    3 T soy sauce
    1 T sesame oil
    1 T oil
    1 T vinegar
    ¼ t pepper
    1/8 t MSG (optional)

Method:

1. Boil 1½ qt water in a 3 qt sauce pan.

2. Put the bean sprouts in the boiling water for a few seconds. If you use soy bean sprouts, they should stay in the boiling water for 1-2 minutes. Rinse and drain.

3. Plunge the bean sprouts in cold, running water until they become thoroughly cold. Drain. Set aside.

4. Boil chicken breast with water for 20 minutes; let cool. Tear the chicken breast into fine shreds.

5. Put the bean sprouts, chicken breast, celery, onion and ginger in a large salad bowl. Add soy sauce, sesame oil, oil, vinegar, MSG and pepper. Mix well. Serve cold.

Add ½ C of carrot shreds if you prefer. The color and nutritive value of the carrots will enrich the whole dish.

Steps 1-4 can be prepared in advance. Wrap the bean sprouts and chicken breast in separate plastic bags until serving time (step 5). *(cont'd)*

Makes 6 servings
Time: 35 minutes

Calories: 647

Carbohydrates: 38 gm

Protein: 56 gm

Fat: 33 gm

(Calculated with mung bean sprouts.)

紅燒鴨

STEWED DUCK
(Hung Chao Ya)

Ingredients:

½ C sherry
2 T honey
8 drops of red food coloring

1 duck, fresh or frozen

10 green onions, cleaned
1½" section of ginger root, crushed
6 T soy sauce
2 t brown sugar
5 C water

Method:

1. Mix the first three ingredients together.
2. Clean and dry the duck inside and outside.
3. In a large bowl, thoroughly baste duck with the sherry mixture. Set aside for 1 hour. Turn duck occasionally for even flavor and color. *(cont'd)*

4. Place duck on a roasting rack in a shallow pan; roast in a 275° oven for 1 hour. This method allows the fat of the duck to drip away.

5. Put the onion and the ginger in the duck cavity.

6. Put the duck in a large deep sauce pan. Add 5 C water, 6 T soy sauce and 2 t brown sugar; bring to a boil.

7. Cook over medium heat until less than 1 C water is left, (about 1½ hours). Turn the duck once or twice during cooking. Serve hot. The duck should be a rich brown color. This dish does not need constant attention while cooking.

Makes 8-10 servings
Time: 2½ hours

Calories: 5034   Carbohydrates: 55 gm
Protein: 244 gm   Fat: 426 gm
(Calculated with 4 pounds of duck. Remember to subtract the calories from the fat that you discard).

SZECHWAN DUCK
(Xiang Su Ya)

Ingredients:

    1 fresh or frozen (thawed) duck, 3-6 pounds
    2 T Szechwan brown peppercorns (Hua Chiao)
    3 T salt
    ½ t onion powder
    ½ t ginger powder
    1 T cornstarch
    Oil for deep-frying

(cont'd)

Method:

1. Stir-roast Hua Chiao in a small sauce pan over medium heat for 2 minutes. Add 3 T salt; roast 2 minutes more. Shake pan constantly to prevent burning while roasting. Let cool.

2. In a covered blender, blend the roasted Hua Chiao for a few seconds or crush the Hua Chiao mixture into a fine powder. This powder is called Hua Chiao powder.

3. Mix 1½ T Hua Chiao powder with ⅓ t onion powder and ½ t ginger powder. Rub the mixture thoroughly on the duck, inside first then outside. Keep the duck in the refrigerator for 6 hours or overnight.

4. Place the duck in a boiling steamer; steam for 1½ hours. Let cool.

5. Mix the cornstarch with 1½ t Hua Chiao powder and rub the mixture evenly on the duck.

6. Heat oil to 375° in a large pan. Deep-fry the duck until brown. Serve hot.

Two ways to serve:

1. Serve whole: Host or hostess will slice the duck meat and serve each person individually. Dip the duck meat in Hua Chiao powder to taste and eat with Lotus Leaf Rolls (recipe on page 129), Chinese bread (recipe on page 238), or dinner rolls.

2. Serve chopped: Chop the duck into 2" square pieces and arrange them on a platter. People will serve themselves and eat in the same manner as above.

This is a very authentic, classic dish, worth trying.

One pound ready to cook duck:

Calories: 1213   Carbohydrates: none
Protein: 60 gm   Fat: 106 gm

SWEET RICE STUFFED DUCK OR
EIGHT PRECIOUS DUCK
(Ba Bao Ya)

Ingredients:

  2 t salt
¼ t pepper
¼ t onion powder
  1 duck, fresh or frozen, about 3-6 pounds
  1 C glutinous rice (sweet rice, about 200 gm)
  3 dried mushrooms, soaked and chopped
  2 T dried shrimp (about 25 gm) soaked and chopped
20 ginkgo nuts, canned (about 25 gm) or dried
    lotus seeds, soaked
  8 water chestnuts, chopped
  2 green onions, minced
  3 T soy sauce
¼ t pepper
½ t sugar
  1 t sherry
½ C Smithfield or Todd's Old Virginia ham
    (about 1 oz) chopped
  1 T minced ginger root
  2 T oil
    Parsley and cherry tomatoes for garnishing

Method:

Prepare ahead:

Soak glutinous rice, mushrooms, dried shrimps and dried
lotus seeds separately in cold water for 1 hour.

(cont'd)

For the Duck:

1. Mix the first three ingredients together.
2. Rub the salt mixture on duck inside and out. Set aside for 1 hour or more.
3. Place the duck in a tier of a steamer; steam for 1½ hours.
4. Cut the back of the duck open (from tail to neck) with a pair of scissors.
5. Carefully remove all the bones (except the bones of the drumsticks and wings) without disturbing the meat and skin.
6. Place the boned duck on a large shallow dish. Set aside.

For the Stuffing:

1. Have the chopped mushrooms, dry shrimp, ham and water chestnuts ready.
2. Have the rice, ginkgo nuts (or lotus seeds), minced onion and ginger root ready.
3. Heat 2 T oil in a medium sauce pan; sauté onion and ginger. Add all the ingredients from steps 1 and 2 plus 3 T soy sauce, ¼ t pepper, 1 T sherry and ½ t sugar; mix well.
4. Add 1½ C water and bring to a boil. Turn to medium heat; cook until water has evaporated. Cover pan, simmer over lowest heat for 15 minutes.

To Cook and Serve:

1. Scoop the cooked rice into the open duck cavity. Steam for 40 minutes.
2. Turn the duck upside down on a large serving platter (the rice will be under the whole duck). Garnish with parsley leaves and cherry tomatoes. Serve hot.

This dish can be prepared in advance. Before serving, steam for 30 minutes or until completely heated.

The leftovers can be reheated in a pan (add a little water in the pan first) or in a steamer. (*cont'd*)

Makes 8-10 servings
Time: 2½ hours

Calories: 4938   Carbohydrates: 190 gm
Protein: 219 gm   Fat: 356 gm

(See page 20)

(Calculated with 3 pounds of duck)

PEKING DUCK
(Bei Jing Ya)

This duck will be eaten with Chinese pancakes, sauce and green onion. You may prepare the pancakes and sauce a few days before roasting the duck.

Ingredients:

    1 duck, fresh or frozen, 3-5 pounds
    ½ C sherry
    2 T honey
    8 drops red food coloring

    2 T soy sauce
    6 T Hoisin sauce
    2 T sugar
    ½ t sesame oil

    2 bunches of green onions

    2 C flour
    1 C boiling water
    1 T sesame oil   *(cont'd)*

Method:

I. For Duck:

1. Mix sherry, honey and food coloring together.
2. Clean and dry the duck inside and outside.
3. In a large bowl, thoroughly baste the duck with sherry mixture. Marinate the duck in the sherry mixture for 1 hour; turn it occasionally for even color and flavor.
4. Place the duck, breast up and uncovered, on a roasting rack in a shallow pan. Keep it in the refrigerator for 24 hours. The skin of the duck will be dried.
5. Roast duck in the oven at 350° for 30 minutes, then reduce temperature to 250° for 1½ hours. Increase temperature to 375° and continue roasting for 10 more minutes.

To serve: Slice the duck skin into strips 1" wide and 2" long, then slice the duck meat the same way. Arrange the pieces on a plate. The crisp side of the skin should be up so that the attractive color will show. Serve hot with Chinese pancakes, sauce and onions. (Sections II, III, IV)

Place a warm pancake on a plate. With a piece of the green onion, spread a thin layer of sauce on the pancake. Put the green onion in the middle of the pancake, add a small portion of the duck skin and meat on the onion. Fold the pancake over the meat and green onion into a cylindrical roll. Hold the roll by hand and eat.

Drying the duck's skin in the refrigerator is more hygienic than drying the skin at room temperature. Bacteria will grow within a few hours at room temperature and some can produce toxin. People will get food poisoning by eating this kind of meat. The skin of the duck will be very crisp after roasting. The drying process contributes to the end result of Peking duck.

One pound ready to cook duck:

(cont'd)

Calories: 1213   Carbohydrates: none
Protein: 60 gm   Fat: 106 gm

II. For Sauce:

1. Mix Hoisin sauce, soy sauce, sugar and sesame oil together.
2. Divide the sauce into small sauce dishes and serve along with sliced duck.

Hoisin sauce can be purchased from Oriental grocery stores.

III. For Green Onions:

1. Cut the white part of the onion about 3" long and discard the root and green top.
2. Cross slit both sides with several slits ½" deep. Soak them in cold water and keep in the refrigerator for 1 hour or more. The ends of the onions will open up like flowers.
3. Drain water off and arrange them in small sauce dishes. Serve the onions along with sliced duck and Chinese pancakes.

IV. For Chinese Pancakes:

1. Pour boiling water slowly into the flour. Mix water and flour with a wooden spoon or a pair of chopsticks into a warm dough.
2. Knead dough for 6 minutes.
3. Form the dough into a cylindrical roll about 1" in diameter.

(cont'd)

4. Cut roll evenly into 1" pieces. Flatten them with the palm of your hand into round cakes, 2" in diameter.

5. Brush a thin layer of sesame oil over one piece of flattened cake and lay another piece over it.

6. Roll the pair of cakes into flat, thin pieces about 5" in diameter.

7. Heat an ungreased skillet over low heat. Cook the rolled cakes until they bubble slightly; turn over and cook the other side for a few seconds.

8. While the cakes are still warm, pull apart into two thin cakes. Pile all the cooked cakes together.

9. Steam cakes for 10 minutes before serving. (The cakes should be piled together while steaming).

The pancakes can be frozen for several weeks when wrapped in a plastic bag.

The nutrition information of the pancakes:

Calories: 965   Carbohydrates: 176 gm
Protein: 24 gm   Fat: 16 gm

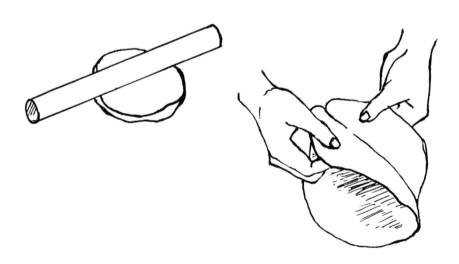

LOTUS LEAF ROLLS
(Ho Ye Juan)

Ingredients:

    1 8 oz tube of ready-to-bake homestyle, chilled
       biscuits (10 pieces)
       Sesame oil for brushing, about 1 t

Method:

1. Roll each biscuit into a 3" long x 1½" wide oval shape.
2. Brush a little sesame oil on rolled biscuit and fold the 3" side over. Repeat the process until the biscuits are used up.
3. Use a fork to make indentations all around the surface of the semi-circle edges.
4. Brush a thin layer of oil on a tier of the steamer. Arrange the rolls neatly, 1" apart, in the tier.
5. Steam over boiling water for 10 minutes.
6. Remove the rolls from the steamer. Stuff them with Szechwan duck meat (or other filling) by opening the rolls at the curved edge. Hold the stuffed roll with your fingers and eat while hot.

Chinese bread dough (page 238) can be used to make Lotus Leaf rolls.

Calories: 670   Carbohydrates: 105 gm
Protein: 17 gm   Fat: 20 gm

seafood

肉絲紅燒魚、 **FISH WITH MEAT SHREDS**
(Rou Si Huang Shao Yu)

Ingredients:

For fish:

    1 t salt
  ¼ t pepper
  ¼ t onion or garlic powder
    1 whole, ready to cook fish, about 1-2 pounds
       (bass, red snapper, pike, trout or white etc.)
       Flour for coating the fish

For pork:

  ¼ C shredded pork (about two ounces)
  ½ T soy sauce
    2 t cornstarch
       Pinch of pepper and MSG

For sauce:

    3 T soy sauce
    3 green onions, shredded
 3-4 dried mushrooms, soaked and shredded
  ⅓ C shredded bamboo shoot
    2 T shredded ginger root
    1 t brown sugar
    1 T cornstarch blended with 1 T water
    1 T sherry
1/8 t MSG
    1 C water
    2 T oil
    1 C oil for deep-frying

(cont'd)

Method:

1. Make 3 crosswise slashes on each side of the fish.
2. Mix the first three ingredients together. Rub the salt mixture on fish and between the slashes. Set aside.
3. Mix shredded meat with ½ T soy sauce and 2 t cornstarch.
4. Heat oil in a wok or frying pan. Coat fish with a thin layer of flour; fry the fish until golden brown. Remove to a serving plate.
5. Pour off oil until about 2 T oil are left in the pan. Stir-fry pork until color turns. Remove to a dish.
6. Sauté onions and ginger in the remaining oil; add mushrooms, bamboo shoots, 3 T soy sauce, 1 T sherry and ½ t brown sugar. Stir and cook for 1 minute.
7. Add 1 C water, blended cornstarch, fried meat and 1/8 t MSG. Bring to a boil. Pour on fried fish evenly. Serve hot.

(Pike is the best fish for this dish)

Makes 4 servings
Time: 45 minutes

Calories: 947   Carbohydrates: 23 gm
Protein: 46 gm   Fat: 73 gm

(Calculated with one pound white bass and 2 T oil for deep-frying.)

Ingredients:

- 1 lb fresh fish, whole or fillets (cod, red snapper, perch, whiting, buffalo, bass, trout or pike)
- 1 t salt
- ¼ t white pepper
- 1/8 t MSG (optional)
- 3-4 dried mushrooms, soaked and shredded
- 1 strip of bacon, cut into small pieces
- 2 green onions, cut into 1" lengths
- 2 T shredded ginger root
- 2 t sherry
- 1 T soy sauce
- 2 T oil or lard

Method:

1. Mix salt, pepper and MSG together. Rub the salt mixture on fish evenly.
2. Place the fish in a shallow dish; garnish with ginger, onion, bacon and mushroom shreds.
3. Pour soy sauce, oil and sherry on the garnishing.
4. Steam for 25 minutes. Serve hot.

Makes 5 servings
Time: 30 minutes

Calories: 672   Carbohydrates: 5 gm
Protein: 83 gm   Fat: 33 gm

(Calculated with cod fish fillet)

SOY SAUCE FISH
(Jiang You Yu)

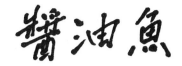

Ingredients:

- 1 lb fish, about 4-5 ready to cook white bass
- 2 T oil
- ½ medium onion, shredded
- 2 thin slices of ginger root
- 3 T soy sauce
- 1 t brown sugar
- 1 t sherry
- ¼ C water

Method:

1. Heat oil in a non-stick pan over high heat. Add fish, cover pan and fry until brown and crisp (takes about 5 minutes).

2. Turn the fish; add onion and ginger. Cover pan and fry until brown.

3. Mix the last four ingredients in a small bowl. Add the mixture to the browned fish; cover and cook until only 1 T juice remains. Serve hot.

This is a basic way to cook fish. The fish will stick to the pan and break if a non-stick pan is not used. Keep the pan covered during the entire cooking time to prevent splashing and smoking from the oil.

If you like a slightly sour flavor, add 1T vinegar to the soy sauce mixture.

Makes 4 servings
Time: 15 minutes

Calories: 489   Carbohydrates: 13 gm
Protein: 35 gm   Fat: 32 gm

Ingredients:

- 4 T soy sauce
- 1 t brown sugar
- 4 thin slices of ginger root
- 1-2 green onions, crushed
- 1-2 cloves of garlic, crushed
- 2 t sherry
- ¼ t pepper
- 1/8 t MSG (optional)
- 1 whole fish, about 1½-2 pounds, cut crosswise into ¾" thick pieces. Use any kind of fish of your choice.
- 1 C oil for deep frying
- 1 bowl of cold water

Method:

1. Mix the first eight ingredients together. Marinate the fish pieces in the sauce mixture for 5-6 hours, turning occasionally.

2. Have a bowl of cold water near your frying pan.

3. Heat oil in a non-stick pan; add fish pieces one by one to the oil. Fry until dark brown. Cover pan while frying to prevent splashing and smoking from the oil.

4. Dip the fish in the cold water for a few seconds right after being fried.

5. Keep the cooked fish pieces in the refrigerator until they are completely cold. Serve cold.

Smoked fish can be easily frozen.

Makes 4-6 servings

Calories: 642   Carbohydrates: 11 gm

(*cont'd*)

Protein: 39 gm   Fat: 48 gm

(Calculated with whole whiting fish and 3 T oil for deep-frying.)

FRIED SMELT FISH
(Zha Zi Yu)

Ingredients:

    1 lb ready to cook smelt fish, fresh or frozen
    1 t salt
  ¼ t pepper
  ¼ t onion powder
    2 T cornstarch
       Oil for deep frying

Method:

1. Mix fish with the next four ingredients.
2. Heat oil in a wok or in a frying pan to 375°. Drop fish one by one into the oil. Fry until light brown.
3. Arrange the fish on a serving plate. Serve hot.
This dish is my little daughter's favorite. I hope some of my readers may also enjoy it.

Makes 6 servings
Time: 20 minutes

Calories: 880   Carbohydrates: 15 gm
Protein: 84 gm   Fat: 52 gm

(Calculated with 3 T oil for deep-frying.)

纸包鱼

FOIL WRAPPED FISH
(Zi Bao Yu)

Ingredients:

- 3 T soy sauce
- ¼ t pepper
- 1 t sherry
- ½ t onion powder
- 4 thin slices of ginger root
- 1 lb cod or sole fillet, cut into 2" sections
- ⅓ C minced ham (about two ounces)
- 3-4 dried mushrooms, soaked and sliced
- 1 T mayonnaise
- ¼ C flour for coating
- 1 T oil for brushing
  Foil, cut into 5" x 5" squares for wrapping.

Method:

1. Mix the first five ingredients together.
2. Marinate fish pieces in the sauce mixture for 2 hours, turning gently from time to time.
3. Coat each fish piece with a layer of flour.
4. Put a piece of fish on a piece of oil brushed foil, spread a thin layer of mayonnaise on the fish, then spread a thin layer of minced ham and mushroom slices on the fish. Wrap up neatly. Repeat.
5. Place the wrapped packages on a baking sheet, ham side up and bake in a preheated 350° oven for 20 minutes. Serve hot.

You may fry the wrapped packages in hot oil but baking is cleaner, easier and less greasy.

Chicken breasts can be cooked in the same manner.

(cont'd)

Makes 4-6 servings

Calories: 901
Protein: 98 gm

Carbohydrates: 27 gm
Fat: 41 gm

(Calculated with cod fish)

FISH FILLET WITH TOMATO SAUCE
(Chao Yu Pian)

炒魚片

Ingredients:

    ¼ t onion powder
  1/8 t MSG (optional)
    1 t salt
    1 T cornstarch
    1 egg white, beaten
    1 t sherry
    1 lb fish fillet, cut into 1" sections
       (cod, sole, pike, flounder or haddock)
    1 T cornstarch for coating the fish pieces
       Oil for deep frying

For Sweet and Sour Sauce:

    ⅓ C sugar
    1 T cornstarch
    ¼ C vinegar
    ¼ C catsup
    ⅓ C water
    ½ t salt
  1/8 t pepper
    ½ t soy sauce
    1 t sesame oil

(cont'd)

For Seasoning:

    2 T oil
    2 slices of ginger root
    ¼ C chopped onion
  3-4 dried mushrooms, soaked and diced
    ¼ C bamboo shoots or water chestnuts, diced
    ¼ C frozen peas, thawed.

Method:

1. Mix the first six ingredients together.
2. Marinate fish pieces in the egg white mixture for 1 hour, turning occasionally.
3. Coat each fish piece with dry cornstarch.
4. Heat oil to 375° and fry fish pieces one by one until light brown. Remove to a serving dish. Set aside.
5. Mix all the ingredients for the sauce together. Set aside.
6. Heat 2 T oil in a frying pan. Brown onion and ginger root; add mushrooms and bamboo shoots. Stir and mix for 1 minute.
7. Add sauce mixture (step 5). Cook until the sauce is thickened.
8. Add green peas and bring to a boil; pour on fried fish. Serve hot.

Makes 6 servings
Time: 40 minutes

Calories: 1363   Carbohydrates: 108 gm
Protein: 80 gm   Fat: 63 gm

(Calculated with cod fish and 2 T oil for deep-frying.)

STEAMED FISH WITH BLACK BEANS
(Dou Chi Zheng Yu)

豆豉蒸魚

Ingredients:

- 1½ lb fresh fish, whole (pike, bass or trout)
- ¼ t salt
- ¼ t pepper
- 1/8 t MSG (optional)
- 3 T black beans (about one ounce)
- 1 T soy sauce
- 2 t sherry
- 2 green onions, shredded
- 1 T shredded ginger root
- 1 T crushed garlic
- 2 T oil or lard

Method:

1. Mix salt, pepper and MSG together. Rub the salt mixture evenly on the fish.
2. Toss the last seven ingredients together gently.
3. Place the fish in a shallow dish. Spread the black bean mixture evenly on the fish.
4. Steam the fish in a boiling steamer for about 20 minutes. Serve at once on its own steaming dish.

Makes 4-6 servings
Time: 25 minutes

Calories: 589
Protein: 64 gm

Carbohydrates: 20 gm
Fat: 31 gm

(Calculated with blue pike.)

141

红烧鱼丸

FISH BALLS IN BROWN SAUCE
(Hung Shao Yu Wan)

Ingredients:

- ½ lb cod, sole, pike, flounder or haddock fillets, cut into small chunks
- 1 t salt
- 1 t sherry
- 1/8 t white pepper
- 1/8 t onion powder
- 1/8 t ginger powder or two thin slices of ginger root
- 2 small eggs
- 1/8 t MSG (optional)
- ⅓ C water
- ½ t baking powder
- 5 water chestnuts, coarsely chopped
- 2 T cornstarch
- 1 C water
- 1 chicken bouillon cube
- 15-20 snow pea pods, washed and cleaned
- 1/8 lb Smithfield or Todd's Old Virginia ham, cut into the size of snow pea pods
- 4 dried mushrooms, soaked and sliced
- 1 T cornstarch blended with ¼ C water
- 1 T sesame oil

Method:

For the fish balls:

1. Put the first nine ingredients in a blender; blend into a smooth paste.

2. Set the fish paste in a bowl; add water chestnuts, cornstarch and baking powder. Mix well. *(cont'd)*

3. Fill a medium sauce pan with water to about half the depth of the pan. Bring to a boil then turn to medium heat.

4. Drop a heaping teaspoonful (use a knife to smooth the surface and help to form a ball shape) of fish paste into the boiling water.

5. Cook 2-3 minutes, several balls at a time. Remove the balls with a slotted spoon to a dish. Set aside.

For the whole dish:

1. Boil together the water, bouillon cube, ham, mushrooms and bamboo shoots for two minutes.

2. Add fish balls and pea pods; mix gently and bring to a boil.

3. Add sesame oil and blended cornstarch. Cook until the sauce thickens. Pour in a serving dish. Shake a little pepper on the top before serving. Serve hot.

Makes 6-8 servings
Time: 40 minutes

Calories: 760   Carbohydrates: 28 gm
Protein: 65 gm   Fat: 41 gm

(Calculated with cod fish)

魚鬆

FLUFFY DRIED FISH
(Yu Song)

Ingredients:

2 T oil
2 6½ ounce cans of tuna (do not drain)
1 onion, minced
3 thin slices of ginger root, minced
¼ t five-spice powder
¼ t pepper
1 t sherry
1 t sugar
1-2 dried hot peppers (optional)

Method:

1. Heat oil in a non-stick pan.
2. Add the rest of the ingredients. Stir-fry constantly until the fish dries and becomes fluffy (about 15-20 minutes). Try carefully to break the fish pieces and prevent burning while stir-frying. Serve cold.

Makes about 2 cups of fluffy fish.

This dried fluffy fish can be kept for 1-2 months in the refrigerator. Chinese use this fish to eat with rice porridge in the morning as breakfast. It is also very good to sprinkle on soup and salad as a source of protein.

Calories: 1368   Carbohydrates: 14 gm
Protein: 91 gm   Fat: 104 gm

BRAISED SHRIMP IN TOMATO SAUCE
(Qie Zhi Ming Xia)

茄汁明蝦

Ingredients:

       1 lb large unshelled shrimp
       3 T oil
       4 T soy sauce
       1 T sugar
       1 T sherry
       2 T minced ginger root
     3-6 green onions, minced
      ¼ t pepper
       3 oz tomato paste
      ¼ C water

Method:

   1. Remove legs from shrimp and devein by cutting the back open. Wash and drain (do not shell shrimp).
   2. Heat oil and fry shrimp for 5 minutes. Add the next six ingredients; stir-fry for 2 minutes.
   3. Add tomato paste and water. Cook for 5 minutes. Stir while cooking. Serve hot.

Makes 6 servings
Time: 15 minutes

Calories: 830   Carbohydrates: 40 gm
Protein: 63 gm   Fat: 45 gm

蝦仁腰果

SHRIMP WITH CASHEWS
(Xia Ren Yao Guo)

Ingredients:

          1 lb shelled shrimp, fresh or frozen
        ½ t salt
        ½ t white pepper
        ¼ t onion powder
      1/8 t MSG (optional)
          1 T cornstarch
          4 T oil
        ½ C freshly roasted cashews
          1 green pepper, diced
      5-6 green onions, minced
          4 slices of ginger root
          1 T sherry
        ½ t salt
          1 T sesame oil

Method:

1. Mix the shrimp with the next four ingredients. Let stand for 30 minutes. Add cornstarch and mix well.

2. Heat oil in a non-stick pan; add shrimp and stir-fry until color turns (about 2 minutes). Remove them to a dish.

3. Sauté the green onions and ginger root in the remaining oil. Add green peppers; stir-fry for 1 minute. Add the last three ingredients and cooked shrimp; mix well.

4. Add roasted cashews to the shrimp and mix well. Serve hot.

Makes 6 servings
Time: 40 minutes

(cont'd)

Calories: 1507　　　　Carbohydrates: 44 gm
Protein: 96 gm　　　　Fat: 106 gm

SHRIMP WITH GREEN PEAS AND TOMATO
(Chao Xia Ren)

炒蝦仁

Ingredients:

 1 lb fresh or frozen shelled shrimp
 2 thin slices of ginger root
 1 t sherry
 ¼ t onion powder
 ¼ t pepper
 1 t salt
1/8 t MSG
 1 T cornstarch
 1 C frozen green peas, thawed (about 5 ounces)
 1 fresh tomato, diced
 1 t cornstarch blended with 1 T of water
 ⅓ C cold water
 4 T oil

Method:

1. Mix shrimp with the next six ingredients. Add cornstarch; mix well.

2. Heat oil in a teflon pan. Spread shrimp evenly in the hot oil. Stir-fry until color turns (about 1½ minutes). Remove the cooked shrimp to a dish.

3. Add peas, water, blended cornstarch and a pinch of salt, MSG, pepper and onion powder to taste in the same pan with the remaining oil; bring to a boil.　　　　　(cont'd)

4. Add cooked shrimp and tomato. Mix well. Serve immediately.

One half to one teaspoon of sesame oil can be added before serving.

Step 1 of the "Method" can be prepared in advance.

Makes 6 servings
Time: 30 minutes

Calories: 1100   Carbohydrates: 42 gm
Protein: 92 gm   Fat: 60 gm

PHOENIX TAILED SHRIMP
(Feng Wei Xia)

Ingredients:

        1 lb large or medium unshelled shrimp
    1½ t salt
      ¼ t onion powder
      ¼ t white pepper
    1/8 t MSG (optional)
      ¼ C cornstarch
        1 C flour and 1 t baking powder
        1 C water
           Oil for deep frying

Method:

1. Mix salt, pepper, MSG and onion powder together. Set aside. *(cont'd)*

148

2. Wash, shell and devein shrimp but leave the shell of the tail on.

3. Sprinkle half of the salt mixture evenly on the shrimp. Set aside.

4. Mix cornstarch, flour/baking powder, water and the other half of the salt mixture together to make a batter.

5. Dry shrimp with a paper towel.

6. Heat oil to 375°.

7. Coat shrimp (except tails) with batter. Fry one by one until golden brown. Serve hot with one of the following dips.

For dipping:

1. Sweet and Sour sauce: Bring to a boil a mixture of 4 T catsup, 4 T sugar, 4 T vinegar, 4 T water and 2 t cornstarch. Stir constantly while cooking.

2. Plum sauce: Buy the prepared one from an Oriental grocery store. Dilute with a little water if it is too thick.

3. Hoisin sauce diluted with a little water.

4. Hua Chiao powder, prepared according to the recipe on page 122, step 2.

Try oysters prepared in the same manner.

This dish can be prepared in advance. Before serving, reheat in a preheated oven at 300° for 5 minutes or until they are completely heated.

Makes 6 servings
Time: 35 minutes

Calories: 1200   Carbohydrates: 121 gm
Protein: 69 gm   Fat: 46 gm

(Calculated with 3 T oil for deep-frying. Dippings are not included in this calculation.)

枕頭蝦餅

Ingredients:

½ lb shelled fresh or frozen shrimp
8-10 water chestnuts, minced
1 strip bacon
1 t cornstarch
¼ small onion, minced
2 slices of ginger root
⅔ t salt
1/8 t white pepper
1 small egg
1/8 t MSG (optional)
6-7 day old white or whole wheat bread
Oil for deep-frying

Method:

1. Mince the shrimp, bacon, onions and ginger root together into a paste.
2. Have the water chestnuts coarsely minced.
3. Mix shrimp mixture with water chestnuts, ⅔ t salt, egg, 1 t cornstarch, MSG and 1/8 t pepper.
4. Trim off and discard the bread crusts. Cut the bread into quarters or 4 triangles. Bread may be flattened with a rolling pin so that is soaks up less oil.
5. Use a small knife to spread the shrimp mixture on bread; mound slightly in the center. Repeat to make 24-28 pieces.
6. Heat oil in a pan to 375°-400°. Deep-fry the shrimp breads, 6-8 pieces at a time, shrimp side first. Turn and fry until both sides are golden brown. Remove with a slotted spoon.
7. Drain and serve hot. *(cont'd)*

You can keep them warm in 200° oven, or re-heat in 300° oven for 10 minutes. They are good to serve as appetizers or hors d'oeuvres.

Calories: 1480   Carbohydrates: 63 gm
Protein: 68 gm   Fat: 101 gm

(Calculated with 6 T oil for deep-frying)

SHRIMP BALLS
(Xia Wan)

蝦 丸

Ingredients:

    10 oz raw shrimp, shelled, fresh or frozen
  1/8 t MSG (optional)
    2 strips bacon, chopped
    1 T sherry
    ¼ small onion
    1 slice of ginger root
  1/8 t pepper
    1 t salt
    1 egg
    2 T water
    ½ t baking powder
    ½ t baking soda
    8 water chestnuts, minced
    2 T cornstarch
    2 C oil for deep frying
       Parsley

(cont'd)

Method:

1. Blend shrimp with the next nine ingredients in a blender to form a smooth paste.
2. Mix the paste with the minced water chestnuts, baking powder, baking soda and cornstarch in a mixing bowl.
3. Heat oil to 375° in a wok or in a deep sauce pan.
4. Gently drop rounded, heaping teaspoonfuls of shrimp paste into the hot oil. Repeat the process until the paste is used up. Fry the shrimp balls until golden brown.
5. Serve hot. Arrange the shrimp balls on a serving plate.

Garnish with green parsley and tomato flowers (made from tomato skin).

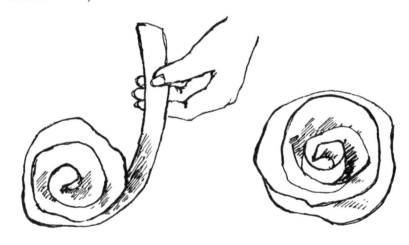

Makes about 40 1" shrimp balls
Time: 35 minutes

Calories: 899
Protein: 64 gm

Carbohydrates: 22 gm
Fat: 62 gm

(Calculated with 3 T oil for deep-frying)

SHRIMP OMELET
(Xia Ren Chao Dan)

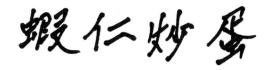

Ingredients:

- ½ lb shelled fresh or frozen shrimp
- 1 t sherry
- ¼ t onion powder
- ¼ t pepper
- ½ t salt
- 2 thin slices of ginger root
- 2 t cornstarch
- 4 eggs, beaten with ½ t salt
- 1-2 green onions, minced
- 4 T oil

Method:

1. Mix shrimp with the next five ingredients. Add cornstarch; mix well.
2. Heat oil in a teflon pan; sauté onion.
3. Add shrimp; stir-fry until color turns (about 1½ minutes).
4. Add egg. When surface of the egg is almost dry, turn and cook for 1 minute. Serve hot.

Try preparing oysters in the same way.

Leftovers can be added to fried rice.

I consider this dish a convenience dish. You could always add it to your table when you have unexpected guests.

Makes 5 servings
Time: 15 minutes

Calories: 1052   Carbohydrates: 10 gm
Protein: 65 gm   Fat: 82 gm

燒龍蝦

Ingredients:

1 T soy sauce
1 T sherry
¼ t pepper
½ t sugar
1 live lobster (about 1½ pounds)
2 T oil
¼ C ground pork (about 1/8 pound)
2 chicken bouillon cubes blended with 1 cup of water
1½ T cornstarch blended with ¼ cup of water
1 egg, beaten
2 t minced ginger root
2 cloves of garlic, minced
2 green onions, minced
1½ T black beans, minced
1 T soy sauce
Salt and pepper to taste

Method:

1. Wash the lobster and cut the head off at the joint. Place the head in a small sauce pan, add ½ C water, cover and cook for ten minutes. Remove the head to a dish and let cool.

2. Cut the claws from the joints, crushing slightly. Cut off the tips of the walking legs and swimmerets. Cut the body and tail lengthwise in half then chop crosswise into 1" pieces (do not shell). Mix with the first four ingredients.

3. Open the cooked head. Pick up the liver (tomalley) and break into small pieces in a small bowl. Discard the shell and remove remaining nonedible ingredients from the head.

(cont'd)

154

4. Heat oil in a medium sauce pan; add the last six ingredients. Stir-fry for ½ minute. Add pork and liver (tomalley). Stir-fry for 1 minute. Add lobster (with the seasonings) and stir-fry for 2 minutes.

5. Add blended bouillon cubes. Cover and cook over medium heat for 5 minutes. Slowly add blended cornstarch. Cook until sauce thickens.

6. Gently add egg and stir for ½ minute. Turn off heat. Serve immediately.

Unshelled large shrimp can be cooked in the same way. When you eat the lobster, suck the juice out first then remove the shell and eat the meat.

Makes 4-6 servings
Time: 20 minutes

Calories: 881   Carbohydrates: 20 gm
Protein: 58 gm   Fat: 60 gm

SWEET AND SOUR LOBSTER
(Tian Suan Long Xia)   甜酸龍蝦

Ingredients:

   ¼ t onion powder
1/8 t MSG (optional)
   2 t salt
   1 T sherry
1½ T cornstarch
   1 lb lobster meat
   4 T oil

(cont'd)

For Sweet and Sour Sauce:

- 1/3 C sugar
- 1 T cornstarch
- ¼ C vinegar
- ¼ C catsup
- 1/3 C water
- ½ t salt
- 1/8 t pepper
- ½ t soy sauce
- 1 t sesame oil

For Seasoning:

- 1 T oil
- 2 slices of ginger root
- ¼ C chopped onion
- ¼ C frozen peas, thawed

Method:

1. Remove lobster meat from shell and cut the meat into 1 inch pieces. Mix the lobster meat with the first five ingredients.
2. Put all the ingredients for the sauce in a small pan. Set aside.
3. Heat 4 T oil in a non-stick pan; stir-fry lobster meat until color turns (about 3 minutes). Remove to a serving dish.
4. Add 1 T oil to the pan. Brown onion and ginger root then add sauce mixture and green peas; cook until the sauce thickens. Pour on the fried lobster. Serve hot.

Makes 6 servings
Time: 30 minutes

Calories: 1555
Protein: 80 gm

Carbohydrates: 110 gm
Fat: 84 gm

SAUTÉED LOBSTER TAIL
(Gan Chao Long Xia)

Ingredients:

- 1 lb lobster tail
- 3 T oil
- 2 T minced ginger root
- 3-6 green onions, minced
- Salt to taste
- 2 t sugar
- ¼ t pepper
- 1 T sherry
- 3 T soy sauce
- ½ C catsup

Method:

1. Wash the lobster tail and cut the tail crosswise into 1" sections.

2. Heat oil; sauté ginger root and onions. Add lobster; stir-fry for 2 minutes.

3. Add the last five ingredients; stir and cook for 5-7 minutes. Serve hot.

One half to one teaspoon of sesame oil can be added before serving.

Makes 4 servings
Time: 20 minutes

Calories: 705
Protein: 26 gm

Carbohydrates: 49 gm
Fat: 50 gm

鮑魚雪豆

ABALONE WITH SNOW PEA PODS AND MUSHROOMS
(Bao Yu Xue Dou)

Ingredients:

- 1 lb abalone, sliced (canned)
- 1/8 lb snow pea pods, washed and cleaned
- 3 Chinese dried mushrooms, soaked and sliced
- 1 C chicken broth
- 1 T cornstarch dissolved in ¼ C water
- 1 t sesame oil
  Salt and pepper to taste
- ¾ C Smithfield or Todd's Old Virginia ham, sliced (about ¼ pound)

Method:

1. Put the abalone slices, chicken broth, mushrooms and ham slices in a sauce pan. Bring to a boil.

2. Add snow pea pods, dissolved cornstarch and sesame oil; cook until the sauce thickens.

Serve hot.

Makes 6 servings
Time: 25 minutes

Calories: 830
Protein: 98 gm

Carbohydrates: 25 gm
Fat: 32 gm

158

HAPPY FAMILY AND REUNION
(Quan Jia Fu)

Ingredients:

1	dried sea cucumber or 1 C soaked and cleaned sea cucumber
1	large egg
½	lb ground pork
¼	lb chicken breast, boned
⅓	C sliced Smithfield or Todd's Old Virginia ham (about two ounces)
½	C bamboo shoots, sliced
4	large dried mushrooms, soaked and sliced
15-20	snow pea pods (about one ounce), cleaned
2	green onions, shredded
2	thin slices of ginger root
1	T sherry
3	T soy sauce
3	C chicken broth
1	T sesame oil
3	T cornstarch blended with 3 T water
1	t cornstarch for mixing with meat
3	T oil
	Salt and pepper to taste
1/8	t pepper
1/8	t onion powder
1	T sherry
1	t cornstarch

For preparing the dried sea cucumber:

1. Put the sea cucumber in a deep sauce pan and add enough water to cover. Cover the pan and bring to a boil. Turn off heat and let the sea cucumber stay in the water for 6

hours. Repeat the same procedure 2-3 times until the sea cucumber has expanded and becomes soft.

2. Wash and discard the loose material from inside the soaked sea cucumber.

3. Boil the sea cucumber with 4 C water and 1" crushed ginger root for 1 minute.

4. Discard water; cut the sea cucumber into 2" x ½" slices.

For the ingredients requiring steaming:

1. Beat egg with a little salt. Spread 1 t oil, with a piece of paper towel, on a hot teflon pan. Pour in egg and tip the pan around so that the egg will cover the pan. Cook over medium heat until the surface of the egg dries. Turn and cook the egg for a few seconds. Remove.

2. Mix pork with 2 T soy sauce, 1 T sherry, 1/8 t pepper, 1/8 t onion powder, 2 T water and 1 t cornstarch.

3. Spread half of the pork mixture on the egg sheet. With the meat inside, roll the egg sheet into a tube. Set aside.

4. Make meat balls ½" in diameter from the other half of the meat.

5. Put the egg tube, meat balls, chicken breast and ham in a shallow dish. Steam for 15 minutes.

Cooking procedures:

1. Slice the steamed chicken breast and ham into 2" x ½" x 1/6" slices.

2. Unroll the egg sheet and cut it into 2" x 1" pieces. Arrange them on a serving dish.

3. Have the chicken, ham, meat balls, snow pea pods, shredded onions, ginger slices, mushrooms, bamboo shoots, chicken broth, sea cucumber, blended cornstarch and sesame oil ready near the stove.

(cont'd)

4. Heat 3 T oil. Sauté the onions and ginger root. Add all the ingredients from the "Procedure" 3. Mix gently and bring to a boil.

5. Pour the cooked food on the egg pieces. Serve hot.

Makes 8-10 servings
Time: 1 hour

Calories: 1514   Carbohydrates: 12 gm
Protein: 81 gm   Fat: 124 gm

(See page 20)

VEGETABLES

炒四季豆   **STRING BEANS, CHINESE STYLE**
(Chaó Se Chi Dou)

Ingredients:

    1 lb fresh string beans
    1 green onion
    2 T soy sauce
    ½ t sugar
    ½ C water
    2 T vegetable oil

Method:

1. Wash the string beans, snapping off the ends. Cut into ½" long pieces.
2. Wash the green onions, discarding the roots and cut into ½" long pieces.
3. Heat oil in a medium sauce pan. Brown onion.
4. Add beans and 2 T soy sauce. Stir-fry for 2 minutes.
5. Add water and sugar. Cover pan and bring to a boil. Reduce to medium heat and cook for 5 minutes. Serve hot.

Variation: add ½ cup mushrooms, bamboo shoot slices or water chestnut slices during step 5. You might need to add ½ T soy sauce to the beans.

Makes 6 servings
Time: 20 minutes

Calories: 420   Carbohydrates: 35 gm
Protein: 10 gm   Fat: 29 gm

**DRY COOKED
STRING BEANS**
(Gan Shao Se Chi Dou)　　乾燒四季豆

Ingredients:

- 1 lb fresh young string beans
- 4 T oil
- 1 T dried shrimp, soaked and minced (about 10 gm)
- 2 T Szechwan mustard pickles (canned)
- 3 green onions, minced
- 2 T minced ginger root
- 1 T minced garlic
- 1 t salt
- ½ t sugar
- 1 T vinegar
- 2 T water

Method:

1. Wash string beans. Remove the tips and strings of the beans and cut into 1½ inch long pieces.

2. Heat oil; sauté minced dried shrimp. Add string beans. Stir and mix for 7 minutes.

3. Add the rest of the ingredients. Stir and mix for 1 minute.

4. Cover the pan and simmer over medium heat for 10 minutes.

5. Increase to high heat. Stir and cook until the sauce is evaporated. Serve hot or cold.

Makes 4-6 servings
Time: 25 minutes

Calories: 680　　　　　　Carbohydrates: 35 gm
Protein: 14 gm　　　　　　Fat: 57 gm

妙白菜

Ingredients:

- 1 lb Bok Choy (green leaf and white-stemmed Chinese cabbage)
- 4 dried mushrooms, soaked and quartered
- 1 green onion, cut into 1" lengths
- ⅓ C sliced ham (about 2 ounces)
- ½ C sliced bamboo shoots
- 1 t salt
- 1 T soy sauce
- 2 t cornstarch blended with 1 T water
- 2 T oil
- ¾ C water

Method:

1. Wash Bok Choy and cut into 1" pieces. Separate white parts from green parts.

2. Heat oil in a pan; brown onion. Add white parts of the Bok Choy, ham, 1 t salt and 1 T soy sauce. Stir-fry for 2 minutes.

3. Add mushrooms, bamboo shoots and ¾ C water. Cook for 5 minutes.

4. Add the green parts of the Bok Choy; mix and cook for 2 minutes.

5. Add blended cornstarch. Mix well. Serve hot.

Makes 6 servings
Time: 20 minutes

Calories: 509   Carbohydrates: 21 gm
Protein: 17 gm   Fat: 41 gm

BROCCOLI CHINESE STYLE
(Chao Jie Cai Hua)

Ingredients:

1 bunch fresh broccoli, about 3 stalks
1 t salt
2 green onions, cut into 1" lengths
3 T vegetable oil
⅓ C cold water

Method:

1. Wash broccoli. Peel the stems and cut into 2 inches long pieces. Cut heavier pieces in halves or quarters.
2. Heat oil in a large deep sauce pan. Brown the onions.
3. Add broccoli and salt. Stir quickly for 1 minute.
4. Cover pan and cook for 1 minute.
5. Add ⅓ C water; cover pan and bring to a boil.
6. Remove lid; stir and cook for 1 minute. Serve hot.

The broccoli will be a bright green color and remain crisp after cooking.

Makes 6 servings
Time: 10 minutes

Calories: 510
Protein: 18 gm

Carbohydrates: 24 gm
Fat: 45 gm

炒菜芽

**BRUSSELS SPROUTS
WITH MEAT SAUCE**
(Chao Cai Ya)

Ingredients:

- 1 lb brussels sprouts
- ¼ C ground beef or pork (about two ounces)
- 2 green onions, shredded
- 2 thin slices of ginger root
- 2 t soy sauce
- 1 t salt
- 1 t sugar
- ½ C water
- 2 T oil

Method:

1. Wash the brussels sprouts and trim off the stems and outer leaves. Cut the sprouts into halves.

2. Heat oil. Sauté the onion and ginger root. Add meat and 2 t soy sauce. Stir and mix for 1 minute.

3. Add brussels sprouts, 1 t salt, 1 t sugar, and ½ cup of water; stir and mix well. Cover pan and bring to a boil. Reduce to medium heat and cook the sprouts for five minutes. Serve hot.

Makes 6 servings
Time: 10 minutes

Calories: 704   Carbohydrates: 34 gm
Protein: 27 gm   Fat: 55 gm

(Calculated with ground beef)

CABBAGE CHINESE STYLE
(Chao Juan Xin Cai)

Ingredients:

    1 small cabbage, 1-2 pounds
    2 T soy sauce
    ¼ onion, chopped
    3 T vegetable oil

Method:

2. Wash cabbage and break the leaves into 2" squares.
2. Heat oil in a large sauce pan. Brown onion.
3. Add cabbage and soy sauce; stir constantly until the leaves are wilted. Serve hot.

Makes 6 servings
Time: 10 minutes

Calories: 503   Carbohydrates: 27 gm
Protein: 7 gm   Fat 43 gm

奶油白菜

CABBAGE WITH CREAM SAUCE
(Nai You Bai Cai)

Ingredients:

   1 lb Chinese cabbage
   ½ C milk
   1 T cornstarch
   2 green onions, shredded
   3 T oil
   1 t salt
   ¼ t pepper
   ½ C chicken broth (canned)
   ¼ t sugar

Method:

1. Separate and wash the cabbage leaves. Cut into 2½" pieces.
2. Mix the milk and cornstarch. Set aside.
3. Heat oil in a pan over high heat. Sauté the onions. Add cabbage and stir for 1 minute.
4. Add the last four ingredients and bring to a boil.
5. Add the milk mixture and cook until the sauce thickens. Serve hot.

Makes 4 servings
Time: 15 minutes

Calories: 563   Carbohydrates: 30 gm
Protein: 11 gm   Fat 47 gm

SWEET AND SOUR CABBAGE
(Tang Cu Bai Cai)

Ingredients:

- 1 lb Chinese cabbage, cut into 2" sections
- ½ t Szechwan peppercorns
- 2 slices of ginger root
- 2-3 red dried hot peppers, halved (optional)
- 2 green onions, cut into 1" sections
- 3 T oil
- 1 T vinegar
- 2 T soy sauce
- 3 T sugar
- 1 t sesame oil
- 1 t sherry
- 1/8 t MSG (optional)
- 1 t cornstarch

Method:

1. Heat oil in a sauce pan. Sauté onions, ginger, Szechwan peppercorns and hot pepper. Add cabbage; stir-fry over high heat for 5 minutes.

2. Mix the last seven ingredients in a small bowl. Pour the sauce on the cabbage. Mix and cook until the sauce thickens. Serve hot.

Makes 4-6 servings
Time 15 minutes

Calories: 639
Protein: 7 gm

Carbohydrates: 53 gm
Fat 47 gm

炒菜花

CAULIFLOWER WITH SOY SAUCE
(Chao Cai Hua)

Ingredients:

1 medium head of cauliflower, about 1 pound
3 T oil
2 T soy sauce
2 green onions, minced
¼ t pepper
¼ C cold water

Method:

1. Wash the cauliflower. Cut the flowerets into 2" x 1" pieces.
2. Heat oil in a deep sauce pan; sauté the onion, add cauliflower and stir-fry for 1 minute.
3. Add soy sauce and stir-fry for one more minute.
4. Add water. Cover pan and cook for 5 minutes. Serve hot.

Makes 4-6 servings
Time: 10 minutes

Calories: 523   Carbohydrates: 28 gm
Protein: 14 gm   Fat 43 gm

172

BABY CUCUMBER SZECHWAN STYLE
(La Huang Gua)

Ingredients:

         1 lb baby cucumber
         1 t salt
         2 T oil
         2 T ginger shreds
     1/8 lb hot peppers, shredded
         1 t Szechwan peppercorns
         2 T sesame oil
         3 T vinegar
         2 T sugar
         1 T soy sauce

Method:

1. Wash and discard both tips of the cucumbers. Quarter the cucumbers lengthwise and mix with the salt. Let it stand for 30 minutes. Drain.

2. Heat oil in a small sauce pan. Saute' ginger, hot peppers and Szechwan peppercorns.

3. Add remaining four ingredients and bring to a boil. Pour the sauce on the cucumber. Let the cucumber strips soak in the sauce for 6 hours. Serve cold.

Makes 6 servings
Time: 15 minutes

Calories: 676   Carbohydrates: 45 gm
Protein: 5 gm   Fat 57 gm

素炒鮮菇 **SAUTÉED FRESH MUSHROOMS**
(Su Chao Xian Gu)

Ingredients:

1 lb fresh mushrooms
3 T oil or butter
1 t salt
1/8 t onion powder
1/8 t pepper

Method:

1. Wash the mushrooms. Cut the larger mushrooms into 2-3 slices.
2. Heat oil over high heat. Add mushrooms and the last three ingredients.
3. Stir and mix for 5 minutes. Serve immediately.

Makes 4-6 servings
Time: 20 minutes

Calories: 498
Protein: 12 gm

Carbohydrates: 19 gm
Fat: 44 gm

BRAISED MUSHROOMS
(Hung Shao Dong Gu)

Ingredients:

1. heaping cup small or medium size dried mushrooms
2 T soy sauce
¼ small onion, chopped
2 thin slices of ginger root
¼ t sugar
1 T oil

Method:

1. Soak the mushrooms in a sauce pan with 3-4 cups of hot water for 1 hour. Drain the mushrooms but keep the water for later use.

2. Put mushrooms and mushroom water in a pan; cover and bring to a boil. Reduce to medium heat and cook until only 2 T of water remains. Serve hot or cold or as hors d'oeuvres.

Constant attention is not needed while cooking this dish.

Makes 6 servings
Time: 30 minutes

Calories: 282
Protein: 13 gm

Carbohydrates: 25 gm
Fat: 15 gm

素炒雪豆

SAUTÉED SNOW PEA PODS
(Su Chao Xue Dou)

Ingredients:

- 1 lb fresh snow pea pods
- 3 T oil
- 1 t salt
- 1/8 t onion powder
- 1/8 t pepper

Method:

1. Wash and snap off the stems and strings from both ends of the snow pea pods.
2. Heat oil in a pan. Add snow peas and the last three ingredients.
3. Stir and mix the peas until the color turns a shining, bright green (about 2 minutes). Serve immediately.

¼ C sliced fresh mushrooms or ¼ C sliced bamboo shoots or both can be added to step 2 of the "Method." If so, you might need to add a little salt to the vegetables.

Makes 4-6 servings
Time: 20 minutes

Calories: 614   Carbohydrates: 54 gm
Protein: 15 gm   Fat: 43 gm

176

SAUTÉED SPINACH
(Su Chao Bo Cai)

素炒菠菜

Ingredients:

    1 lb fresh spinach
    ¾ t salt
    2 green onions, shredded
    3 T oil

Method:

1. Wash spinach and break it into 2" pieces.
2. Heat oil in a deep sauce pan. Sauté onion.
3. Add spinach and salt; stir-fry until the spinach is wilted.
Serve hot.

Makes 4-6 servings
Time: 10 minutes

Calories: 499   Carbohydrates: 21 gm
Protein: 15 gm   Fat: 43 gm

蝦米蘿蔔
DRIED SHRIMP AND TURNIPS
(Xia Mi Lu Bo)

Ingredients:

- 1½ lb turnip
- 4 T dried shrimp (about 50 grams)
- ¼ onion, chopped
- 1/8 t pepper
- 2 T soy sauce
- 3 T oil
- 1 C water

Method:

1. Soak dried shrimp in 1 C of hot water for ½ hour. Drain shrimp but keep the water for later use.
2. Peel off the turnip skin, rolling-cut into 1" pieces.
3. Heat oil in a pan; brown onion and shrimp. Add turnip and soy sauce. Stir-fry for 2 minutes.
4. Add shrimp water and pepper. Cover pan and bring to a boil. Turn to medium heat and cook until about ¼ C water remains. Serve hot.

Chinese cabbage and Chinese radish may be cooked with dried shrimp in the same manner.

Makes 6 servings
Time: 30 minutes

Calories: 700
Protein: 38 gm

Carbohydrates: 39 gm
Fat: 43 gm

ASPARAGUS SALAD
(Liang Ban Lu Sun)

涼拌蘆筍

Ingredients:

    1 lb fresh asparagus
    3 T soy sauce
    1 t sesame oil
    1 T oil
    1 T vinegar
1/8 t pepper
1/8 t MSG (optional)
  ¼ t onion powder

Method:

1. Cut off the tough parts of the asparagus. Wash.
2. Boil 1½ qt of water in a 3 qt sauce pan.
3. Drop the asparagus in the boiling water and cook for 1 minute.
4. Drain and plunge the asparagus into cold running water until it is thoroughly chilled. Drain well.
5. Rolling-cut the asparagus into 1" lengths.
6. Mix the last seven ingredients in a small bowl.
7. Combine the asparagus with the sauce mixture before serving. Garnish with some egg shreds (recipe on page 242) on the salad if you desire.

The dressing (step 6 of the "Method") can be prepared in advance and kept in a jar. It may be re-used once by adding a little salt.

Makes 6 servings
Time: 15 minutes

Calories: 262
Protein: 8 gm

Carbohydrates: 17 gm
Fat: 18 gm

蝦米拌芹菜

CELERY AND DRIED SHRIMP SALAD
(Xia Mi Ban Qin Cai)

Ingredients:

- 1 lb celery hearts
- 4 T dried shrimp (about 50 grams)
- 1 C water
- 3 T soy sauce
- 2 t sesame seeds oil
- 1 T vegetable oil
- 1 T vinegar
- ¼ t pepper
- ¼ t onion powder

Method:

1. Put the dry shrimp and water in a small sauce pan. Bring to a boil. Turn off heat and let stand for 20 minutes. Drain.

2. Wash celery stalks and cut into 1½" pieces.

3. Combine the last six ingredients together in a small bowl.

4. Put the celery and dry shrimp in a serving dish. Pour the sauce mixture on the celery and shrimp. Mix well. Serve immediately.

Makes 6 servings
Time: 25 minutes

Calories: 400
Protein: 36 gm

Carbohydrates: 18 gm
Fat: 21 gm

COUNTRY SALAD
(Liang Ban Sun Cai)

Ingredients:

1 bowl of salad made up of the vegetables of your own choice such as lettuce, endive, escarole, spinach, watercress, radish, celery, cucumber, tomato, carrot, cauliflower and green pepper.

For Dressing:

¼ C vinegar
2 t salt
¼ t pepper
2 T chopped onions
½ C vegetable oil
¼ C sesame oil (optional)

Method:

1. Break up or slice the salad vegetables into the size you prefer.
2. Put all the ingredients for the salad dressing in a jar. Cover tightly and shake for 2 minutes. This dressing will be enough for several bowls of salad.
3. Add enough dressing to make the leaves glisten. Toss gently until every piece is coated with dressing before serving.

Calories: 1458   Carbohydrates: none
Protein: none   Fat: 165 gm

(The only nutrition information that can be calculated is ¾ C of oil.)

PICKLED SPICY VEGETABLES
(Pao Cai)

Ingredients:

For the brine:

¼ C salt
5 C boiling water (more or less, depending upon the size of the jar used)
1-2 T Szechwan peppercorns (Hua Chiao)
1 inch ginger root, peeled and crushed
6 cloves of garlic
1 T sherry
5 dried hot peppers

Fresh vegetables:

5 baby cucumbers, whole
½ C turnip sticks
½ C carrot sticks
3 young cabbage leaves, cut into 2" x 2" squares
½ C young green string beans, cut into 1½" lengths
A large glass jar

Method:

For the brine:

1. Put salt in the cleaned glass jar. Pour in boiling water and let cool.

2. Add the remaining ingredients for the brine to the salted water.

For the pickled vegetables:

1. Wash and dry vegetables with paper towel. Drop the
(cont'd)

182

vegetables carefully into the jar. Be sure the brine covers all the vegetables.

2. Cover and keep the jar in the refrigerator for 3 days. Remove the vegetables with a clean fork or chopsticks to a dish and serve.

The brine can be used many times. Add a little salt when putting new vegetables in.

PICKLED MUSTARD GREENS
(Xue Li Hung)

Ingredients:

    1 lb fresh mustard greens
    1 T salt

Method:

1. Wash mustard greens and let dry for half a day or overnight on a rack.

2. Put the mustard greens in a mixing bowl. Sprinkle salt evenly on the greens.

3. Mix and squeeze with your hands until the greens are wilted. Pack tightly in a glass jar. Keep in the refrigerator for 2 days before using.

This pickled mustard can be used in many dishes. See recipes on pages 27, 76, and 209.

The pickled greens can be kept in a covered glass jar in the refrigerator for as long as two weeks.

Calories: 98   Carbohydrates: 18 gm
Protein: 10 gm   Fat: 2 gm

辣椒醬

HOT PEPPER PASTE
(La Jiao Jiang)

Ingredients:

 1 lb fresh hot peppers, green or red
 1 C vegetable oil
 1 oz garlic (about 1 whole bulb)
 2 slices of ginger root
 1 T salt
 ¼ C black beans (optional)

Method:

1. Wash the hot peppers and discard the stems.
2. Cut the peppers into halves.
3. Crush the garlic cloves and discard the skin.
4. Put the hot peppers, garlic and the rest of the ingredients in a blender and blend for 2 minutes.
5. Pour the blended hot pepper mixture into a deep sauce pan; cover and bring to a boil over high heat. Reduce to low heat and simmer, covered for ½ hour. Stir the paste occasionally while cooking.

Keep the hot pepper paste in a clean, covered jar in the refrigerator and use a small portion at each time.

This as a basic hot pepper paste recipe. You can add black beans, soaked and minced dry shrimp, mushrooms, etc. as a variation.

Calories: 2102   Carbohydrates: 37 gm
Protein: 6 gm   Fat: 220 gm

HOME GROWN BEAN SPROUTS
(Fa Dou Ya)

Materials:

    3 T (heaping) mung beans
    1 C water
    1 3 pound empty coffee can or any other kind of
      large can
      cheese cloth or paper towel

Method:

1. Wash the beans. Soak them in 1 C cold water for 6 hours or overnight.

2. Punch several holes in the bottom of the coffee can. Spread 3 layers of wet cheese cloth or paper towel in the bottom of the can.

3. Spread an even layer of soaked beans on the cheese cloth. Cover the can with a plate or a piece of cardboard.

4. Set the can on a bowl (in order to catch the dripping water) and store it in any dark and warm place.

5. Sprinkle a few tablespoons of water on the beans three to four times a day.

6. After 4-5 days, the bean sprouts will grow to 2 inches long. Pull the bean sprouts gently off the cheese cloth. Put them in a sink filled with cold water.

7. Gather the clean bean sprouts which are floating on top of the water. These fresh and tender bean sprouts are ready for you to make your favorite dishes.

Three tablespoonsfuls of dry beans will grow approximately 1 pound of bean sprouts.

Soy bean sprouts are grown in the same way as mung bean sprouts. The mung bean sprouts are more popular in the United States.

(cont'd)

There are several things you might keep in your mind when growing your own bean sprouts:

1. All the equipment should be very clean; if not, bacteria will grow and the beans will rot before they sprout.

2. The beans should always be kept moist but not soaked in water.

3. The beans should be kept in a dark and warm place.

4. If the beans fail to grow after 5 days or grow only less than 1" long (it will happen very often), throw the whole thing away and try again. Do not be discouraged!

5. It is not necessary to use a coffee can to grow bean sprouts. Any utensil in your kitchen will do, as long as it serves the purpose. Be imaginative!

One pound of mung bean sprouts:

Calories: 159   Carbohydrates: 30 gm
Protein: 17 gm   Fat: 1 gm

麵筋

WHEAT GLUTEN (VEGETABLE STEAK)
(Mian Jing)

This is a kind of vegetable protein from wheat flour. Because the nutritive value is very high, the vegetarian people in China always use this protein (as well as soy bean curd) in their diet. It does take a little time to prepare but I hope you will find it worthwhile to try.   (cont'd)

Ingredients:

    2¾ C all purpose flour
      1 C cold water
      1 t salt
        Oil for deep-frying

Method:

1. Put flour, water and salt in a mixing bowl and mix to form a dough.

2. Knead the dough on a lightly floured board for 10 minutes.

3. Return the dough to the mixing bowl. Cover with a dampened cloth. Store in the refrigerator for 6 hours or overnight.

4. Divide the dough into four portions.

5. Rinse one portion of the dough under a light stream of cold water (a strong force of water will wash away the gluten). Use your hands to rub and squeeze the dough gently. After a little while you will feel and see a sticky substance (gluten) left on the dough while the white starch is running away.

6. Continue squeezing and washing until all the white starch is washed away; meanwhile you have to carefully try to gather and keep the gluten. Keep the gluten in a small bowl with cold water.

7. Repeat the process until all the dough is washed into gluten.

8. Divide the gluten into 15-20 ball shaped pieces.

9. Heat oil to 375°. Deep-fry the gluten balls one by one until golden brown. They will puff up to three times bigger than the original ones.

The fried gluten can be frozen for a long time without losing flavor when wrapped in a plastic bag.　　　　(cont'd)

To cook: please see the recipes

Vegetarian's Delight (page 189)
Braised Wheat Gluten (page 188)
Meat Stuffed Gluten Balls (page 66)
Braised Pork Hock (page 82)
Braised Beef (page 53)

Calories: 507   Carbohydrates: none
Protein: 33 gm   Fat: 42 gm

(Calculated with the protein content of the sifted flour and
3 tablespoons of oil for deep-frying.)

紅燒麵筋   **BRAISED WHEAT GLUTEN**
(Hung Shao Mian Jing)

Ingredients:

20 balls of fried wheat gluten (page 186)
 1 green onion, cut into 1" pieces
 2 thin slices of ginger root
 2 T soy sauce
1/8 t pepper
 ½ t brown sugar
1½ C water

Method:

1. Put all the ingredients in a sauce pan; cover and bring to
a boil.
2. Reduce heat to low. Simmer until only a few tablespoons
of water remain.   *(cont'd)*

188

Serve hot or cold, as a main dish, appetizer or as hors d'oeuvres.

Makes 4 servings
Time: 30 minutes

Calories: 543	Carbohydrates: 7 gm
Protein: 35 gm	Fat: 42 gm

VEGETARIAN'S DELIGHT
(Su Shi Jin)

Ingredients:

- 10 balls of fried wheat gluten (see recipe for making wheat gluten on page 186)
- 2 oz dried bean curd sticks, soaked and cooked
- 20 dried lily buds (golden needles), soaked, washed and knotted (see page 212)
- 5 dried mushrooms, soaked and quartered
- 10 dried black wood ears, soaked and broken into small pieces
- ½ oz dried sea weed, soaked and cut into 2" pieces
- 10 ginkgo nuts (Bok-Gor nuts), canned
- 10 thin slices of lotus root, canned
- 8 water chestnuts, sliced
- ½ C bamboo shoots, sliced
- 4 T soy sauce
- 1/8 t salt
- 1/8 t pepper
- 1 t brown sugar
- 1 t sesame oil

(cont'd)

2 green onions, cut into 1" pieces
2-4 slices of ginger root
1½ C water
1/8 t MSG (optional)
2 T oil
1 t soda

Method:

1. Soak the dried bean curd sticks with 1 t soda in hot water for 1 hour; drain. Add fresh cold water and bring to a boil. Drain and cut into 1" long pieces. Set aside.

2. Soak dried lily buds, mushrooms, sea weed and wood ears in separate bowls with hot water for 30 minutes. Drain, wash and cut.

3. Have the sliced lotus root, water chestnuts, bamboo shoots, ginkgo nuts, wheat gluten, ginger root, onion and all the other ingredients ready.

5. Heat oil; sauté onions and ginger. Add all the ingredients except sesame oil. Cover the pan and cook over medium heat for 15 minutes or until water is almost evaporated. Stir occasionally while cooking.

6. Add sesame oil; mix well. Serve hot.

Makes 6-8 servings

(See page 20)

BEAN CURD [to fu]

To Fu, being a vegetable protein, has a high nutritional value and contains no cholesterol. It is made from specially processed soy beans. Long before the existence of written records, Chinese used To Fu in their diet. It is the most important soy bean food in supplying protein nutrition in China.

The use of soy beans and soy bean products in the United States covers only a very short period of recent time and is rather unfamiliar to most people. But the great potential which soy beans have for meeting the protein requirements of man as a direct source of protein is a great one. A United Nations Publication (1968) says "No other single source of unconventional protein could contribute so greatly and so promptly towards closing the protein gap." The following figures will give a further illustration: One acre of soy beans will provide enough protein to sustain a moderately active man for 2,224 days. This figure may be compared with the number of days of protein produced by one acre of wheat, 877 days; or of corn, 354 days. Even the latter values are considerably higher than the 77 days supply of protein which could be derived from one acre of land used to support beef cattle.

The soy bean and its products used as foodstuffs are a rather new introduction into the Western world. This section is devoted to introducing Americans to the many possibilities of utilizing such important nutritional contents found in the soy bean, and hopefully will encourage people to discover a new and tasty eating experience. Meanwhile, we hope that by promoting the eating of To Fu, we may help to prevent the protein crisis which might be one of the problems we will encounter in the future.

BEAN CURD
(Dou Fu)

豆腐

Ingredients:

   1 C soy beans
   ½ t calcium sulfate dissolved in ⅓ C of water for
     soft To Fu or ½ t calcium chloride dissolved
     in ⅓ C of water for a firmer To Fu or 2 T vinegar
     diluted in ½ C of water or 1 t Epsom salt
     dissolved in ½ C of water

Method:

1. Soak soy beans in cold water overnight. It will yield three cups of soaked soy beans.

2. Put three layers of cheese cloth in a colander. Set the colander in a large mixing bowl (or in a large deep sauce pan). Set aside.

3. Blend one cup of soaked soy beans with three cups of cold water in a blender for two minutes.

4. Pour the blended soy beans into the colander. Squeeze out the liquid (soy milk) and discard the solids. Repeat the process until three cups of soy beans are blended and squeezed.

5. Place the soy milk in a large, deep sauce pan (I will call this pan, "pan A"); bring to a boil. Stir the milk while it cooks to prevent scorching.

6. Put the dissolved calcium sulfate (or calcium chloride or vinegar or Epsom salt) into another large pan (I will call this pan, "pan B").

7. Pour the boiling soy milk in pan A into pan B then pour back into pan A.

8. Pour the soy milk back and forth between the two pans until the soy milk starts to coagulate (about 5-6 times). Let it set for 10 minutes. (cont'd)

9. Line a colander with two layers of cheese cloth (a square wooden case can also be used). Pour the coagulated soy milk into the colander. The bean curd will remain on the cheese cloth as the whey is strained away.

10. Gently press out the excess water from the bean curd. It is ready to use or store when cold.

Makes about ¾ pound of To Fu.

If the soy milk does not coagulate (after step 8), cook over medium heat, stirring constantly until it does coagulate.

Calcium sulfate (also called Plaster of Paris), calcium chloride and Epsom salt are sold in chemical stores, drug stores or in some hardware stores.

Bean curd (To Fu) is available in some supermarkets, health food stores, or in Oriental grocery stores. It can be kept fresh for ten days in the refrigerator by keeping it submerged in water in a covered jar. Change the water once every two days.

Firmer To Fu is good for fried and dried To Fu.

One pound of bean curd:

Calories: 327   Carbohydrates: 11 gm
Protein: 35 gm   Fat: 19 gm

FRIED BEAN CURD (TO FU), PLAIN
(You Dou Fu)

Ingredients:

2 lb fresh bean curd
1-2 C oil for deep frying   *(cont'd)*

Method:

1. Cut bean curd into 2" x 2" x 1" pieces.
2. Towel dry the bean curd pieces.
3. Heat oil in a wok or in a deep sauce pan. Fry bean curd, a few pieces at a time until golden brown.

The fried bean curd is ready to use. (See pages 200 and 206)

Fried bean curd can be frozen for 6 months. Fried bean curd can be bought in an Oriental grocery store by weight. Most Oriental grocery stores sell cooked and flavored fried bean curd in cans. It is ready to eat.

Calories: 1154   Carbohydrates: 22 gm
Protein: 71 gm   Fat: 94 gm

(Calculated with 4 T oil for deep frying.)

DRY BEAN CURD
(Dou Fu Gan)

Wrap 2-3 pounds of bean curd in a large piece of cheese cloth. Put a cutting board or any flat article on the wrapped bean curd. Add a heavy stone on top of the board and leave for several hours or overnight.

Unwrap the cheese cloth. The bean curd will be dried and ready to make your favorite dishes.

(See recipes on pages 196 and 198)

Calories: 654   Carbohydrates: 22 gm
Protein: 71 gm   Fat: 38 gm

(Calculated with 2 pounds of To Fu.)

五香豆干

SPICED DRY BEAN CURD
(Wu Xiang Dou Fu Gan)

Ingredients:

- 1 recipe of dried bean curd
- ½ t five-spice powder
- 2 T soy sauce or to taste
- 1 C water

Method:

Combine all the ingredients in a sauce pan; cover and bring to a boil. Reduce to low heat and simmer for 20 minutes. Turn occasionally. If it becomes too dry while cooking, add a little water.

To serve: Cut the bean curd into small pieces; serve hot or cold, as a snack or as one of the ingredients of many dishes.

Calories: 674
Protein: 71 gm

Carbohydrates: 24 gm
Fat: 38.2 gm

什錦豆腐

BEAN CURD WITH ASSORTED MEATS AND VEGETABLES
(Shi Jin Dou Fu)

Ingredients:

- 1 lb bean curd, cut into 1" x 2" x ½" slices
- 2 slices of ginger root
- 2 green onions, shredded
- 1½ t salt
- 4 dried black mushrooms

(cont'd)

196

½ C sliced bamboo shoots
¼ lb shelled shrimp, fresh or frozen
¼ lb pork loin, sliced
2 t cornstarch
2 t sherry
1 T soy sauce
1/8 t pepper
1/8 t MSG
2 t cornstarch blended with ¼ C of water
1 t sesame oil
4 T oil

Method:

1. Soak mushrooms in one cup of hot water for 1 hour; squeeze out excess water and cut into four pieces. Save the mushroom water for later use.

2. Mix shrimp with 1 t sherry, ¼ t salt and 1 t cornstarch. Mix the pork slices with the same amount of seasoning. Set aside.

3. Heat oil in a non-stick pan, add onions, ginger and bean curd slices. Spread 1 t salt evenly on bean curd. Lightly brown both sides of the bean curd.

4. Add the mushroom water, mushrooms and bamboo shoot slices; bring to a boil.

5. Add shrimp and meat slices one by one to the pan; stir and mix for 1 minute.

6. Add soy sauce, pepper, MSG and bring to a boil. Stir in the blended cornstarch and sesame oil; cook until the sauce thickens. Serve hot.

Makes 6 servings
Time: 30 minutes

Calories: 1261   Carbohydrates: 28 gm
Protein: 82 gm   Fat: 97 gm

豆干炒肉絲

**MEAT WITH
DRY BEAN CURD**
(Dou Gan Chao Rou Si)

Ingredients:

½ lb pork or beef, shredded
2 T soy sauce
¼ t pepper
1 t sherry
1 t cornstarch
½ recipe dried bean curd, shredded, about 1 cup
  (recipe on page 195)
2 green onions, shredded
1 t shredded ginger root
½ C minced mustard greens, ½ C shredded carrot or
  ½ C shredded celery
1 t brown sugar
1 T soy sauce
3-4 T oil

Method:

1. Mix the first five ingredients together. Set aside.

2. Heat oil in a teflon pan; stir-fry meat until color turns. Remove and set aside.

3. Put bean curd shreds, green onions, ginger root and 1 T soy sauce in the remaining oil; stir and mix for 3 minutes.

4. Add cooked meat, sugar and mustard greens (celery or carrots). Stir and cook for 2 minutes. Serve hot.

The leftovers can be reheated by stir-mixing in a pan for a few minutes.

Dried bean curd may be obtained from an Oriental grocery store or you can make it in your home (recipe on page 195). It can be refrigerated for a few days or kept in the freezer for quite a long time.   *(cont'd)*

198

Makes 6 servings
Time: 30 minutes

Calories: 1355   Carbohydrates: 28 gm
Protein: 76 gm   Fat: 106 gm

(Calculated with pork butt)

BEAN CURD FOO YOUNG
(Fu Rong Dou Fu)

Ingredients:

       1 lb bean curd
      ¼ lb ground pork butt
      ¼ lb shelled shrimp, fresh or frozen, minced
      ½ C minced bamboo shoots
       1 t salt
       1 t sherry
      ¼ t pepper
      ¼ t onion powder
      ½ t sesame oil
    1/8 t MSG (optional)
    3-4 dried mushrooms, soaked and shredded
      ⅓ C finely shredded Smithfield or Todd's Old
         Virginia ham (about 2 ounces)
       1 green onion, shredded
       2 slices of ginger root, finely shredded
       1 t salt
      ¼ t pepper
       1 egg white
       1 t sesame oil

(cont'd)

Method:

1. Mix ground pork with the next eight ingredients.
2. Place the bean curd in a mixing bowl. Add the last four ingredients, using a fork to break up the bean curd. Mix thoroughly.
3. Put half of the bean curd mixture in a deep heat-proof dish; add the pork mixture. Evenly spread the other half of the bean curd on top of the pork. Gently press the surface until flat.
4. Spread the shreds of the mushrooms, ham, green onion and ginger root on top of the bean curd. Steam in a steamer for 40 minutes. Serve hot.

Makes 6 servings
Time: 50 mintues

Calories: 989
Protein: 90 gm

Carbohydrates: 15 gm
Fat: 63 gm

油豆腐釀肉

**MEAT STUFFED FRIED
BEAN CURD (TO FU)**
(You Dou Fu Niang Rou)

Ingredients:

- ½ lb ground beef or pork
- ¼ C water chestnuts, minced
- 3-4 dried mushrooms, soaked and minced
- ¼ C minced onions
- 1 t sherry
- 1 T soy sauce
- 1 t minced ginger root
- 1/8 t pepper

1/8 t MSG (optional)
½ recipe of fried been curd, home made (recipe on page 194) or prepared bean curd from the Oriental grocery store
1 green onion, cut into 1" long strips
2 slices of ginger root
2 T soy sauce
1 t brown sugar
1 C water

Method:

1. Mix the first nine ingredients together. This mixture will be the filling.

2. Slit an opening on the side of a fried bean curd; stuff with a teaspoon of meat. Repeat the process until all the fried bean curds are stuffed.

3. Put the stuffed fried bean curds and the last five ingredients in a sauce pan; bring to a boil.

4. Reduce to medium heat and cook until only a few tablespoons of water are left.

This dish does not need constant attention while cooking.

The fried bean curds can be kept for a few days in the refrigerator or several weeks in the freezer when wrapped in a plastic bag. The cooked stuffed bean curds can be made one or two days in advance. Heat in a pan before serving. Leftovers can be reheated and served.

Makes 6-8 servings
Time: 30 minutes

Calories: 1270   Carbohydrates: 26 gm
Protein: 80 gm   Fat: 95 gm

(Calculated with ground beef)

素菜豆腐 BEAN CURD WITH VEGETABLES
(Su Cai Dou Fu)

Ingredients:

- ½ lb bean curd, sliced (2" x 1" x ½")
- 3 T oil
- 2 green onions, shredded
- 2 slices of ginger root
- ¼ lb ham, sliced (2" x 1" x 1/6")
- ½ lb Bok Choy
- ½ lb fresh tomatoes, cut into cubes
- 3 T soy sauce
- ¼ t pepper
- 1/8 t MSG (optional)
- ½ t sugar

Method:

1. Wash Bok Choy and cut into 1" sections. Separate the white parts from the green parts. Set aside.
2. Heat oil in a non-stick pan; sauté the onions and ginger root. Add the ham and stir-fry for 1 minute.
3. Add bean curd, the white parts of the Bok Choy and the last five ingredients; bring to a boil. Turn to low heat and cook for five minutes.
4. Add the green parts of the Bok Choy and cook over high heat for one minute. Mix and serve.

Fresh or dried mushrooms can be added in this dish.

One half to one teaspoon of sesame oil can be added before serving.

Makes 4-6 servings
Time: 15 minutes

(cont'd)

Calories: 981   Carbohydrates: 32 gm
Protein: 45 gm   Fat: 78 gm

BLACK BEAN TO FU
(Dou Shi Dou Fu)

Ingredients:

    1   lb bean curd, diced
    2   green onions, minced
    2   thin slices of ginger root, minced
    1   oz black beans (about 3 T) finely chopped
    ½   C ground pork or beef (about 4 ounces)
    3   T oil
    2   T soy sauce
  1/8   t pepper
  1/8   t MSG (optional)
    ¼   t sugar

Method:

1. Heat oil in a non-stick pan; sauté the onions, ginger root and black beans.
2. Add meat and stir-fry for two minutes.
3. Add bean curd dices and the last four ingredients. Mix and bring to a boil; stir while cooking. Serve hot.

Makes 4-5 servings
Time: 15 minutes

Calories: 1090   Carbohydrates: 18 gm
Protein: 60 gm   Fat: 87 gm

(Calculated with ground beef.)

辣豆腐

Ingredients:

 1 lb bean curd, diced
 ⅓ C steamed and minced Smithfield or Todd's
    Old Virginia ham (about 2 ounces)
 1 T cornstarch blended with 2 T of water
 3 chicken bouillion cubes, softened in 1 C of water
 1 T oil
 1 t (or more) hot pepper paste (page 184)
 2 green onions, minced
 1 t minced ginger root

Method:

1. Put the last five ingredients in a sauce pan; bring to a boil.

2. Add the bean curd and again bring to a boil. Cover and cook over medium heat for 2 minutes.

3. Add blended cornstarch and cook until the sauce thickens.

4. Remove the cooked bean curd to a serving dish. Sprinkle it with minced ham and serve hot.

One half to one teaspoon of sesame oil can be added before serving.

Makes 6 servings
Time: 15 minutes

Calories: 720
Protein: 49 gm

Carbohydrates: 20 gm
Fat: 51 gm

MA PO TO FU (BEAN CURD)
(Ma Po Dou Fu)

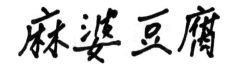

Ingredients:

1 lb bean curd, diced
½ lb ground pork or beef
1 T minced garlic
2 green onions, minced
1 T minced ginger root
¼ t pepper
3 T soy sauce
1 t cornstarch blended with ¼ C cold water
½-1 t hot oil or hot sauce (optional)
1 T sesame oil
1 T oil
1/8 t MSG (optional)

Method:

1. Mix meat with 1 T soy sauce and 1 t cornstarch.
2. Heat oil. Add meat, minced garlic, onion and ginger. Stir-fry for 2-3 minutes. Separate meat while stir-frying.
3. Add diced bean curd, 2 T soy sauce, ¼ t pepper and MSG; stir and mix for ½ minute (salt to taste).
4. Cover pan and bring to a boil.
5. Add well blended cornstarch and 1 T sesame oil (hot sauce); stir and cook until sauce thickens. Serve hot.

Makes 6 servings
Time: 10-15 minutes

Calories: 1215   Carbohydrates: 25 gm
Protein: 76 gm   Fat: 92 gm

(Calculated with pork butt)

红烧油豆腐

SOY SAUCE FRIED BEAN CURD (TO FU)
(Hung Shao You Dou Fu)

Ingredients:

- ½ recipe of fried bean curd, plain (page 194)
- 3 T soy sauce, or to taste
- 2 green onions, cut into 2" lengths
- 1 t brown sugar
- 3 thin slices of ginger root
- 1 C water

Method:

1. Put fried bean curd, onions, ginger root, soy sauce and water in a sauce pan. Cover and bring to a boil.
2. Turn to low heat and simmer for 20 minutes.
3. Add brown sugar and cook over medium heat until only a few tablespoons of water are left. Serve hot or cold.

One half to one teaspoon of sesame oil can be added before serving.

Fried bean curd can be frozen before or after it is cooked. It can be cooked with meat or used in soup etc.

Fried bean curd can be obtained in an Oriental grocery store. Most Oriental stores sell cooked and flavored fried bean curd in cans which are imported from China or Japan. They are very delicious.

Calories: 627
Protein: 37 gm

Carbohydrates: 19 gm
Fat: 47 gm

COLD BEAN CURD
(Liang Ban Dou Fu)

Ingredients:

    1   lb bean curd
    3   T soy sauce
    2   green onions, finely minced
    1   t minced ginger root
1/8   t pepper
    1   t sherry
    2   T oil
1/8   t MSG (optional)
    1   t hot pepper paste (optional, see page 184)

Method:

1. Rinse the bean curd; dry it in a paper towel and place in a bowl.

2. Add all the remaining ingredients to the bean curd. Break up the bean curd mixing it thoroughly with the seasonings. Serve cold.

Minced ham or soaked and minced Chinese mushrooms may be added.

One half to one teaspoon of sesame oil can be added before serving.

Makes 4-5 servings
Time: 10 minutes

Calories: 617   Carbohydrates: 16 gm
Protein: 37 gm   Fat: 47 gm

波菜豆腐

SPINACH WITH BEAN CURD
(Bo Cai Dou Fu)

Ingredients:

    1   lb bean curd, sliced (2" x 1" x ½")
    2   green onions, shredded
    2   slices of ginger root
    3   T oil
    ½   lb fresh spinach
    2   t cornstarch blended in ¼ C of water
    ½   t salt
    1/8 t pepper
    1/8 t MSG (optional)
    ¼   t sesame oil
    2   chicken bouillon cubes softened in ½ C water
    ½   t sugar

Method:

1. Wash spinach; drain well and cut into 1" sections.
2. Heat oil; saute' the onions and ginger root. Add bean curd and the last six ingredients. Bring to a boil.
3. Turn to low heat, cover and cook for 5 minutes.
4. Add spinach; bring to a boil.
5. Add blended cornstarch and bring to a boil. Serve hot.

Makes 6 servings
Time: 15 minutes

Calories: 814   Carbohydrates: 29 gm
Protein: 44 gm   Fat: 62 gm

BEAN CURD WITH PICKLED GREENS
(Xian Cai Dou Fu)

醎菜豆腐

Ingredients:

- 1 lb bean curd, sliced (2" x 1" x ¾")
- ¼ lb beef flank steak, sliced (2" x 1" x 1/8")
- 1 T soy sauce
- ¼ t onion powder
- ¼ t pepper
- 1 t cornstarch
- 3-4 T oil
- 2 green onions, shredded
- 2 slices of ginger root
- 1 T soy sauce
- ¼ recipe of pickled mustard greens (page 183), minced
- ½ t sugar
- 1/8 t MSG (optional)
- Salt and pepper to taste

Method:

1. Mix beef with the next four ingredients. Set aside.
2. Heat oil in a non-stick pan. Add beef and stir-fry until color turns (1-2 minutes). Remove.
3. Add the onions and ginger root in the remaining oil and sauté for a few seconds.
4. Add bean curd slices and the last five ingredients; bring to a boil.
5. Turn to low heat and cook for 2 more minutes. Add cooked meat; gently stir and mix well. Serve hot.

One half to one teaspoon of sesame oil can be added before serving. *(cont'd)*

Makes 6 servings
Time: 15 minutes

Calories: 925
Protein: 63 gm

Carbohydrates: 23 gm
Fat: 67 gm

**BAMBOO SHOOTS
WITH BEAN CURD**
(Dou Fu Sun Pian)

Ingredients:

- ¾ lb bean curd, sliced (2" x 1" x ½")
- ½ lb Smithfield or Todd's Old Virginia ham,
  sliced (2" x 1" x 1/6")
- 1 T oil
- 2 green onions, shredded
- 2 slices of ginger root
- 1 T cornstarch blended with 2 T water
- ¾ C sliced bamboo shoots
- 3-4 dried mushrooms, soaked and sliced
- 1 C mushroom water
- 2 T soy sauce
- 1/8 t MSG (optional)
- 1/8 t pepper
- 1 t sherry
- ½ t sesame oil (optional)

Method:

1. Soak the dried mushrooms in one cup of hot water for 30 minutes. Squeeze the soaked mushrooms dry and cut into slices. Save the mushroom water for later use.

2. Heat oil in a pan; saute the onions and ginger root. Add sliced ham and stir-fry for one minute.

3. Add the last eight ingredients and bring to a boil. Turn to low heat, cover and cook for 5 minutes.

4. Add blended cornstarch; cook and stir until the sauce thickens. Serve hot.

Makes 4-6 servings
Time: 15 minutes

Calories: 1151   Carbohydrates: 23 gm
Protein: 74 gm   Fat: 84 gm

HOT AND SOUR TO FU SOUP
(Suan La Tang)

Ingredients:

   ¼ C shredded pork butt (about 1/8 pound)
   4 chicken or beef bouillon cubes
   4 C water
   1 t cornstarch
   1 T soy sauce
   1 T dried black wood ear, soaked and washed
 15 dried lily buds, soaked and washed
   1 large dried mushroom, soaked and washed
   ¼ C bamboo shoots, shredded
   ½ lb To Fu (bean curd), shredded
   1 egg, beaten
   2 T vinegar
   1 t sesame oil
   ¼ t pepper
   1 t hot sauce (optional)
   2 T cornstarch blended with 4 T water
   1 green onion, minced

(cont'd)

Method:

1. Mix pork with 1 T soy sauce and 1 t cornstarch. Set aside.
2. Soak lily buds, wood ears and mushroom in separate small bowls of hot water for 40 minutes.
3. Cut mushroom into shreds; wash wood ears thoroughly; have the lily buds drained and knotted (see below) and the bamboo shoots ready.
4. Put 4 cups water and 4 bouillon cubes in a medium sauce pan and bring to a boil.
5. Add pork, mushroom, wood ear, lily buds and bamboo shoots. Bring to a boil again.
6. Add To Fu shreds; bring to a boil once more.
7. Stir in 2 T vinegar and 2 T blended cornstarch. Cook until the soup thickens.
8. Turn off heat. Stir in beaten egg and 1 t sesame oil. Add hot sauce (if you prefer) and ¼ t pepper.
9. Pour in a tureen. Sprinkle green onion on the surface of the soup. Serve hot.

Makes 4-6 servings
Time: 20 minutes

Calories: 534   Carbohydrates: 31 gm
Protein: 37 gm   Fat: 32 gm

(See page 20)

BEAN CURD SOUP
(Dou Fu Tang)

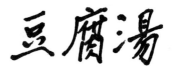

Ingredients:

- ½ lb bean curd, sliced (2" x 1" x ½")
- ¼ lb pork butt or chicken breast, sliced (2" x 1" x 1/8")
- 1 T soy sauce
- 1/8 t onion powder
- 1/8 t pepper
- 1 t cornstarch
- 3 C chicken broth
- 2 slices of ginger root (optional)
- ¼ lb celery cabbage or spinach, cut into 1" sections
  Few drops of sesame oil (optional)

Method:

1. Mix pork (or chicken breast) with the next four ingredients. Set aside.
2. Put the chicken broth and ginger root in a deep sauce pan; bring to a boil.
3. Add the bean curd slices; bring to a boil.
4. Add the meat slices one by one and bring to a boil.
5. Add the vegetables and again bring to a boil. Add sesame oil and serve hot.

Makes 4-6 servings
Time: 15 minutes

Calories: 606 Carbohydrates: 23 gm
Protein: 58 gm Fat: 32 gm

蝦仁豆腐

SHRIMP BEAN CURD
(Xia Ren Dou Fu)

Ingredients:

- ¾ lb bean curd, diced
- ¼ lb fresh or frozen shelled shrimp
- 1 t sherry
- 1/8 t onion powder
- 1/8 t pepper
- ⅓ t salt
- 2 t cornstarch
- 3-4 T oil
- 2 green onions, minced
- 1 t minced ginger root
- 2 t cornstarch blended in ⅓ C of water
- 2 medium-size dried wood ears, soaked and cut into ½" squares
- ¼ C frozen peas, thawed (about 1 ounce)
- 1/8 t MSG
- ½ t salt

Method:

1. Mix shrimps with the next five ingredients. Set aside.
2. Heat oil in a non-stick pan; add shrimp and stir-fry until color turns (about 1-2 minutes). Remove to a dish.
3. Sauté green onions and ginger root in the remaining oil. Add bean curd and the last four ingredients; bring to a boil.
4. Add blended cornstarch and cooked shrimp. Stir and cook until the sauce thickens. Serve hot.

A few drops of sesame oil may be added before serving.

Makes 4-6 servings
Time: 15 minutes

(cont'd)

Calories: 793
Protein: 47 gm

Carbohydrates: 25 gm
Fat: 57 gm

(See page 20)

BEAN CURD WITH FISH IN EARTHENWARE POT
(Sa Quo Yu Tou)

Ingredients:

  1 lb fish head (any kind of large fish of your choice)
  1 T Hua Chiao powder (see page 122, step 2)
  1 T cornstarch
     Oil for deep-frying
  1 inch ginger root, crushed
  4 green onions, shredded
  1 T sherry
  1 t pepper
  1 t salt, or to taste
1-2 oz bean thread, soaked and drained
 ½ lb bean curd, sliced (2" x 1" x ½")
1/8 t MSG (optional)
 ½ t sugar

Method:

1. Wash the fish head (discarding the gills) and rub it thoroughly, inside and out, with Hua Chiao powder. Let it set for 2 hours.

2. Rub the fish head with cornstarch. Set aside. *(cont'd)*

3. Heat oil in a deep pan and deep-fry the fish head until brown and crisp.

4. Pour out all but 3 T of oil.

5. In an earthenware pot add 2 cups of water, the fried fish (with its oil) and the last nine ingredients. Cover and bring to a boil. Turn to low heat and simmer for 40 minutes. Serve hot in the same earthenware pot.

One half to one teaspoon of sesame oil can be added before serving.

An earthenware pot is the authentic cookware for this dish but any regular cooking pot can be used.

Whole fish instead of fish head may be used in this recipe.

Makes 6 servings
Time: 1 hour

Calories: 1266   Carbohydrates: 17 gm
Protein: 57 gm   Fat: 108 gm

(Calculated with whole haddock, also see page 20)

BEAN CURD WITH SMOKED FISH
(Xun Yu Dou Fu)

Ingredients:

    1 lb bean curd, sliced (2" x 1" x ¾")
    ¼ lb smoked fish of your choice
    3 T oil
  4-6 green onions, shredded
  4-6 slices of ginger root
    2 t cornstarch blended with 2 T of water
    ¼ t pepper
    1 t sherry
    ½ t sugar
    1 C water
  1/8 t MSG (optional)
    Salt to taste (Some smoked fish is very salty and
additional salt does not need to be added)

Method:

1. Heat oil; sauté the onions and ginger root.
2. Add smoked fish; stir for 1 minute.
3. Add water, bean curd and the last six ingredients. Cover
and bring to a boil. Turn to low heat and cook for 8 minutes.
4. Add blended cornstarch and cook until the sauce thickens. Serve hot.

Makes 6 servings
Time: 15 minutes

Calories: 1097   Carbohydrates: 21 gm
Protein: 76 gm   Fat: 79 gm

(Calculated with hard-smoked herring.)

RICE, noodles and chinese steamed BREAD

Ingredients:

    1 C rice
    2 C cold water

Method:

1. Put rice and water in a small sauce pan. Cover and bring to a boil over high heat.

2. Remove lid, but continue boiling over medium-high heat until water has completely evaporated.

3. Cover pan tightly. Turn heat to the lowest setting. Simmer rice for 20 minutes. Turn off heat but do not open lid until time to use the cooked rice.

DO NOT STIR THE RICE OR OPEN THE LID WHILE SIMMERING!

If amount of rice is doubled, do not double the amount of water but add enough water to the pan to cover rice 1".

Time: 25 minutes
Makes 6-8 servings

Calories: 670   Carbohydrates: 149 gm
Protein: 12 gm   Fat: 1 gm

220

STEAMED RICE
(Zheng Fan)

Ingredients:

    1½ C rice
        Cold water

Method:

1. Soak rice in 2-3 qt. cold water for 1 hour.
2. Rinse and drain the soaked rice.
3. Spread a layer of cheese cloth in a tier of a steamer. Spread the rice on the cheese cloth.
4. Cover the tier and steam the rice over boiling water for 40 minutes. Serve hot.

Time: 50 minutes
Makes 6-8 servings

Calories: 1005
Protein: 18 gm

Carbohydrates: 224 gm
Fat: 2 gm

雞丁炒飯

Ingredients:

- ½ lb chicken breast, diced
- 2 eggs, beaten
- 1 C frozen peas and carrots, thawed (about 5 ounces)
- 3-4 dry mushrooms, soaked and diced or 1 cup diced fresh mushrooms
- 3 C cooked rice, hot (see page 229)
- ½ t salt
- 1/8 t MSG
- 1 green onion, minced
- 1 T soy sauce
- 1 t cornstarch
- 3 T oil

Method:

1. Mix diced chicken with 1 T soy sauce and 1 t cornstarch.
2. Heat 2 T oil in a teflon pan; scramble the eggs. Remove.
3. Add 1 T oil. Stir-fry chicken and onion for 2 minutes, separating the chicken pieces as you stir.
4. Add peas and carrots, mushrooms, hot rice, ½ t salt and 1/8 t MSG; stir and mix for 3 minutes. Add scrambled eggs. Mix well. Serve hot.

One half to one teaspoon of sesame oil can be added before serving.

Makes 6 servings
Time: 40 minutes

Calories: 1502
Protein: 67 gm

Carbohydrates: 170 gm
Fat: 60 gm

222

RICE WITH CRAB
OR LOBSTER MEAT
(Xie Rou Chao Fan)

蟹肉炒飯

Ingredients:

    3 C cooked rice, hot (see page 229)
    6 oz crab or lobster meat, canned
  ½ C bamboo shoots, diced
 3-4 dried mushrooms, soaked and diced
    2 eggs, beaten with a little salt
  ¼ medium onion, chopped
  ¾ t salt
    3 T oil
  ½ C frozen peas and carrots, thawed
  ¼ t pepper
 1/8 t MSG (optional)

Method:

1. Tear crab or lobster meat into shreds with hands or with a fork.

2. Heat 2 T oil in a teflon pan; scramble the eggs. Set aside.

3. Add 1 T oil and brown the onion. Add crab (or lobster) meat; stir and mix for 1 minute.

4. Add rice, bamboo shoots, mushrooms, peas and carrots, ¾ t salt, ¼ t pepper and 1/8 t MSG. Stir and mix for 5 minutes.

5. Add scrambled eggs and mix well. Serve hot.

One half to one teaspoon of sesame oil can be added before serving.

Makes 6-8 servings
Time: 40 minutes

Calories: 1269   Carbohydrates: 161 gm
Protein: 43 gm   Fat: 47 gm

蝦仁炒飯

Ingredients:

    3 C cooked rice, hot (see page 229)
   ¼ lb shelled shrimp, fresh or frozen
   2 eggs, beaten
   1 t cornstarch
 2-3 dried mushrooms, soaked and diced or ½ C diced
       fresh mushrooms
   ½ C frozen peas, thawed
   ½ C diced bamboo shoots or water chestnuts
   2 green onions, minced
 1/8 t pepper
 1/8 t MSG
   ¾ t salt
   3 T oil

Method:

1. Mix shrimp with ¼ t salt, a pinch of MSG, pepper and 1 t cornstarch. Set aside.

2. Heat 2 T oil in a teflon pan; scramble eggs. Set aside.

3. Add 1 T oil and stir-fry shrimp for 2 minutes.

4. Add mushrooms, peas, water chestnuts, onion, rice, 1/8 t pepper, ½ t salt, and 1/8 t MSG. Stir and mix for 3 minutes.

5. Add scrambled eggs and cooked shrimp, mixing well. Serve hot.

One half to one teaspoon of sesame oil can be added before serving.

Makes 6-8 servings
Time: 35 minutes
(cont'd)

Calories: 1354   Carbohydrates: 161 gm
Protein: 46 gm   Fat: 57 gm

SAUSAGE RICE
(La Chang Chao Fan)

腊腸炒飯

Ingredients:

    3 C cooked rice, hot (see page 229)
    3 Chinese sausages, about 100 gm
    ¼ t salt and pepper, or to taste
    2 green onions, minced
    2 eggs, beaten
    1 T oil

Method:

1. Slant-slice sausages into ¼" thick pieces.
2. Heat oil in a teflon pan; sauté sausage pieces for 5 minutes. Remove.
3. Scramble eggs in the remaining oil. Set aside.
4. Add onion, rice, salt and pepper. Stir and mix for 3 minutes.
5. Add scrambled eggs and sautéed sausage. Mix well. Serve hot.

Makes 6 servings
Time: 30 minutes

Calories: 1565   Carbohydrates: 155 gm
Protein: 41 gm   Fat: 85 gm

叉燒炒飯

RED BROILED PORK RICE
(Cha Shao Chao Fan)

Ingredients:

3 C cooked rice (see page 229)
¼ recipe broiled pork, sliced (recipe on page 86)
15-20 fresh snow pea pods, washed and cleaned
(about two ounces)
2 green onions, shredded
2 T soy sauce
1/8 t pepper
1/8 t MSG
2-3 T oil

Method:

1. Heat oil in a teflon pan; add onions and pork slices. Stir-fry for 5 minutes.

2. Add rice, soy sauce and MSG; stir and mix for 3 minutes. Add snow peas. Cook and mix for 2 minutes. Serve hot.

Makes 6-8 servings
Time: 30 minutes

Calories: 1553   Carbohydrates: 161 gm
Protein: 54 gm   Fat: 75 gm

CURRIED BEEF RICE
(Ka Li Fan)

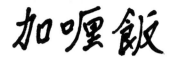

Ingredients:

   3 C cooked hot rice (see page 229)
   1 lb beef (boneless chuck, shank etc.) diced into
      ½" cubes
   1 onion, diced
   2 T curry powder mixed with 2 T water
   3 C water
   2 T soy sauce
  ½ t salt
  ¼ t pepper
   2 medium sized potatoes, peeled and diced
 10 oz frozen peas and carrots (1 box)
   1 T oil
   2 T cornstarch blended with 4 T water

Method:

1. Mix curry powder with 2 T water; have the diced onion ready.
2. Heat oil in a medium sauce pan. Brown the onions. Add the beef, curry paste, 2 T soy sauce, ¼ t pepper, ¼ t salt; stir and cook over medium heat for 2 minutes.
3. Add 3 C water; cover and bring to a boil. Reduce to low heat and simmer for ½ hour or until the meat becomes tender.
4. Add potatoes. Cook over medium heat until the potato becomes soft and about 2 C sauce is left with the meat. If the water evaporates too fast, add a little water to make up 2 cups.
5. Add peas and carrots; bring to a boil.
6. Add blended cornstarch; stir until the sauce thickens.

(cont'd)

7. Put the hot rice in a serving dish. Pour the curried beef on rice. Serve hot. This dish does not need constant attention while cooking.

Makes 8 servings
Time: 1 hour

Calories: 2396   Carbohydrates: 242 gm
Protein: 101 gm   Fat: 105 gm

(Calculated with beef chuck. See page 20)

什錦炒飯

**FRIED RICE WITH ASSORTED
VEGETABLES AND HAM**
(Shi Jin Chao Fan)

Ingredients:

- 3 C cooked rice, hot. See the method of boiling rice (next page)
- 2 eggs, beaten with a pinch of salt
- 3 T oil
- ¼ C chopped onion
- 1 C frozen peas and carrots (about five ounces), thawed
- ½-1 C ham, (about two-four ounces), cut into the size of the frozen carrots
- 1 C minced celery
- ½ t salt
- 1/8 t pepper
- 1/8 t MSG

(cont'd)

228

Method:

1. Heat oil in a teflon pan. Scramble eggs. Set aside.
2. Brown the onions in the remaining oil. Add the last six ingredients; mix well. Cover the pan and bring to a boil.
3. Combine the hot rice and scrambled eggs. Mix well. Serve hot.

One half to one teaspoon of sesame oil can be added before serving.

Boiled Rice:

Ingredients:

    1 C long grain rice
    2 C cold water
   ½ t salt

Method:

1. Put the rice, salt and water in a small sauce pan; bring to a boil.
2. Remove lid but continue boiling water until water has completely evaporated.
3. Cover pan tightly. Turn the heat to the lowest setting and simmer the rice for 20 minutes. Do not open the lid until it is time to use the rice. It will make 3 cups of cooked rice.
DO NOT STIR THE RICE OR OPEN THE LID WHILE SIMMERING!
If amount of rice is doubled, do not double the amount of water but add enough water to the pan to cover rice 1".

Makes 6 servings
Time: 40 minutes

Calories: 1457   Carbohydrates: 169 gm
Protein: 39 gm   Fat: 69 gm

腊八粥

EIGHTH OF THE TWELVE MONTH RICE CHOWDER
(La Ba Zhou)

Ingredients:

- 1 C rice
- 7 C water
- 4-5 dried mushrooms, soaked and sliced
- ½ C bamboo shoots, sliced
- ½ C ham (about two ounces)
  sliced, or cooked chicken breast, shredded
- 6 chicken bouillon cubes
- 20 ginkgo nuts, canned (about 25 grams)
- 30 dried lily buds, soaked, washed and knotted
  (see page 212)
- 1 lb Bok Choy, cut into 1" sections
- 1 T sesame oil
- 1/8 t MSG (optional)
  Salt and pepper to taste

Method:

1. Put rice and water in a large, deep sauce pan; cover and bring to a boil. Reduce to a low heat and simmer for 40 minutes.

2. Add mushrooms, bamboo shoots, ham and chicken bouillon cubes; cover and simmer for 10 minutes. Stir occasionally.

3. Add ginkgo nuts and lily buds; cover and simmer for 10 minutes. Stir occasionally.

4. Add Bok Choy and 1 T sesame oil; cook and stir for 5 minutes. Serve hot.

Peeled and diced taro may be added in step 2.

In the southeast region of China, this special kind of chowder is served to indicate that the Chinese New Year is near. They start to prepare for the New Year very early—cleaning, scrubbing, cooking and making new clothes for every member of the family.

Makes 8-10 servings
Time: 1 hour

Calories: 1148   Carbohydrates: 182 gm
Protein: 38 gm   Fat: 29 gm

(See page 20)

HOME-MADE NOODLES
(Mian Tiao)

Ingredients:

    2　C flour
    1　large egg
   ½　C cold water
       Cornstarch for flouring the board　　*(cont'd)*

Method:

1. Mix the first three ingredients in a large mixing bowl. Knead the dough on a floured board until very smooth (10-15 minutes).

2. Put the dough back into the mixing bowl; cover with a damp cloth and let it stand for 20-30 minutes.

3. Place the dough on a floured board and knead for 5 minutes more.

4. Roll the dough out into a 1/6" thick sheet. Flour the dough from time to time to prevent its sticking.

5. Fold the rolled-out dough and cut into fine strips.

6. Unfold the strips by fluffing up with your fingers. Cook the noodles in rapidly boiling water for 5 minutes before using.

Makes about one pound of noodles.

Calories: 920   Carbohydrates: 176 gm
Protein: 30 gm   Fat: 8 gm

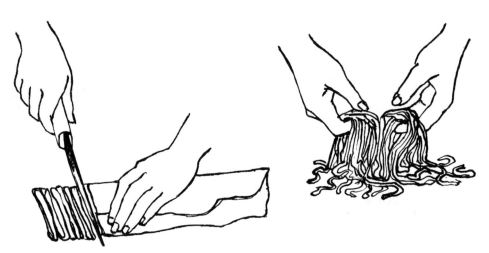

EGG NOODLES
(Dan Mian)

Ingredients:

    2 C flour
    3 large eggs
    1 T cold water
    ½ t salt
    Cornstarch for flouring the board

Method:

1. Mix the first four ingredients in a large mixing bowl. Knead the dough until very smooth (about 10-15 minutes).
2. Put the dough back into the mixing bowl and cover the bowl with a damp cloth. Let it stand at room temperature for 20-30 minutes.
3. Place the dough on a floured board; knead for 5 minutes. Roll the dough with a rolling pin into a 1/6" thick sheet. Flour the dough and board from time to time to prevent sticking.
4. Fold the dough and cut into fine strips.
5. Unfold the strips by fluffing up with your fingers. The noodles are ready to use now.

Makes about one pound of noodles.

Calories: 1080   Carbohydrates: 176 gm
Protein: 42 gm   Fat: 20 gm

涼拌麵

Ingredients:

- 5 oz thin spaghetti noodles
- 1 T sesame oil
- ½ lb chicken breast
- ½ lb fresh bean sprouts
- 1 C celery hearts, shredded
- 1 carrot, shredded
- 2-3 dried mushrooms, soaked and shredded
- 2 green onions, finely shredded
- 1 T finely shredded ginger root
- 3 T soy sauce
- ¼ t pepper
- 1 T vinegar
- 2 T oil
- 1 t sesame oil
- 2 cloves of garlic, crushed
- ¼ t MSG
- Salt and pepper to taste

Method:

1. Drop the bean sprouts in boiling water for 1 second; rinse under cold water until the bean sprouts become cold. Drain.

2. Add noodles to 2-3 qts of rapidly boiling water. Add 1 T salt to the water and cook for 10 minutes. Drain in a colander, then rinse under cold water until the noodles become completely cold. Drain and chill.

3. Mix noodles with 1 T sesame oil and 1 T soy sauce. Chill.

4. Boil chicken breast in water for 20 minutes; remove and

(cont'd)

let it cool to room temperature. Tear the cooked chicken breast into fine shreds. Chill.

5. Add the shredded celery, carrots, mushrooms, green onions, chicken and sprouts to the noodles.

6. Mix 2 T soy sauce and the last six ingredients in a small bowl. Pour on the noodles and vegetables. Mix well. Serve cold.

Steps 1-4 can be prepared 1 day in advance. Put each ingredient in a separate bag and keep in the refrigerator.

These noodles are especially good in the summertime.

Makes 8-10 servings
Time: 40 minutes

Calories: 1436
Protein: 68 gm

Carbohydrates: 141 gm
Fat: 65 gm

FRIED NOODLES (CHOW MEIN)
SOFT TYPE
(Shi Jin Chao Mian)

什錦炒麵

Ingredients:

- ½ lb meat, shredded (beef, pork or chicken breast)
- 1 T sherry
- ¼ t pepper
- 1/8 t onion powder
- 1 t minced ginger root
- 1 t cornstarch
- 5 oz noodles, thin spaghetti or home made noodles (recipe on page 231)
- 1 C celery or bamboo shoots, shredded (or fresh bean sprouts) *(cont'd)*

½ lb celery cabbage, shredded
2 carrots, shredded
½ onion, shredded
¼ lb fresh mushrooms, shredded, or 3-4 dried mushrooms, soaked and shredded
4 T soy sauce
1/8 t MSG (optional)
5 T oil

Method:

1. Mix meat with 1 T soy sauce and the next five ingredients.

2. Add noodles to 2 to 3 qt. rapidly boiling water. Add 1 T salt to the water; cook for 10 minutes (if home-made noodles are used, cook for 5 minutes only). Drain in a colander. Rinse thoroughly under cold water.

3. Heat 4 T oil in a teflon pan. Stir-fry meat until color turns. Remove the meat to a dish.

4. Add noodles, onions, 2 T soy sauce, a pinch of pepper and MSG to the same pan. Stir-fry for 3 minutes.

5. Add carrots; mix for 1 minute then add celery cabbage, shredded celery, mushrooms, 1 T soy sauce, 1/8 t MSG and 1T oil. Stir-fry for 2 more minutes. Add cooked meat and mix well. Serve hot.

One half to one teaspoon of sesame oil can be added before serving.

Makes 8 servings
Time: 35 minutes

Calories: 1674
Protein: 79 gm

Carbohydrates: 143 gm
Fat: 84 gm

(Calculated with beef flank steak)

FRIED NOODLES (CHOW MEIN)
CRISP TYPE
(Liang Mian Huang)

二面黄

Ingredients:

- ½ lb meat (beef, pork or chicken), shredded
- ¼ t pepper
- ¼ t onion powder
- 2 slices of ginger root
- 1 t sherry
- 1 T cornstarch
- 8 oz pure egg noodles (see recipe on page 233)
- 7 T oil
- ½ lb celery cabbage, shredded (or 2 C celery cabbage and 1 C of bamboo shoots and 1 C of fresh bean sprouts)
- ¼ lb fresh mushrooms, shredded or 3-4 dried mushrooms, soaked and shredded
- 3 T soy sauce
- 2 C water
- 2 T cornstarch dissolved in 2 T water
- 1/8 t MSG (optional)
- 4 green onions, shredded

Method:

1. Mix meat with 1 T soy sauce and next five ingredients.

2. Add noodles to 3 qts of rapidly boiling water. Add 1 T salt to the water and cook for 5 minutes. Drain and rinse thoroughly under cold water until the noodles become cold.

3. Heat 6 T oil in a teflon pan. Add noodles to the pan and shape them into a round cake. Fry the cake until the bottom is golden brown; turn over and brown the other side. Remove.

4. Add 1 T oil. Stir-fry meat until color turns. Remove.

5. Put the last seven ingredients in the pan. Stir and cook until the cabbage becomes tender. Mix with cooked meat and pour over the noodle cake and serve hot.

Keep the fried noodles (step 3) in a heated oven while cooking the sauce. (steps 4-5).

One half to one teaspoon of sesame oil can be added before serving.

Makes 8 servings
Time: 45 minutes

Calories: 1957
Protein: 82 gm

Carbohydrates: 133 gm
Fat: 121 gm

(Calculated with beef flank steak)

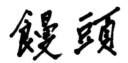

CHINESE STEAMED BREAD
(Man Tou)

Ingredients:

¼ oz dry yeast (one package)
⅓ C sugar, if you prefer a sweeter taste use ½ cup
2 C water
1 t salt
¼ C oil or butter
5 C all purpose flour
1 T baking powder

Method:

1. Mix yeast and sugar in a small bowl; add ½ C warm water to soften the yeast.

2. Put 1½ C warm water in a large mixing bowl. Add yeast mixture and the rest of the ingredients. Blend well.

3. Cover the bowl with a damp towel. Let the dough rise until double in bulk (about one to two hours, depending upon the temperature).

4. Place the dough on a floured board and knead for 5-8 minutes.

5. Divide the dough into 4 portions. Form each portion into a round bun or a bread loaf.

6. Place a piece of wax paper (a little bit bigger than the shape of the loaf) under each loaf. Let rise again until double in bulk (about one hour).

7. Arrange the bread loaves with the wax paper in the tiers of a steamer. Steam for 15 minutes. Serve hot.

Always boil the water before steaming the bread. If your steamer has two tiers, put two loaves in each tier and steam at the same time. The bread slices best when it is cold. Re-steam the cold bread slices for 3 minutes before serving.

The bread can be frozen for months when wrapped in a plastic bag. I always make a lot of bread at one time and freeze the extra loaves.

Chinese steam bread is very difficult to make. It requires great skill. Most people in China buy the ready-made bread. I have developed this recipe, which is so good and so easy, that any American or Chinese housewife can make it in her own kitchen. The Chinese bread made in my kitchen has been overwhelmingly enjoyed by guests and friends of "old-China hands." I am very proud of this recipe.

Calories: 2862
Protein: 63 gm

Carbohydrates: 509 gm
Fat: 60 gm

EGGS

Ingredients:

    2 eggs
    ¼ t salt
    ½ t oil

Method:

1. Beat eggs with salt. Set aside.
2. Spread ¼ t oil evenly in a teflon pan (with a small piece of kitchen paper towel).
3. Heat pan; pour half of the beaten egg in the pan and tip the pan so that a thin layer of egg covers the bottom.
4. Cook over medium heat until the surface is dried.
5. Turn and cook for a few seconds. Remove. Cook the other portion of the egg in the same manner.
6. Pile the cooked egg sheets together and cut into 4 strips. Pile the strips and slice them into fine shreds.

These egg shreds make a colorful garnish for salads, soups and other dishes. The egg shreds can be frozen; thaw before using.

Calories: 181   Carbohydrates: none
Protein: 12 gm   Fat: 14 gm

TOMATO SCRAMBLED EGGS
(Fan Qie Chao Dan)

Ingredients:

    2 medium-size tomatoes, cut into wedges
    4 large eggs, beaten with half of the salt
    1 green onion, cut into 1" long pieces
    1/8 t pepper
    ¾ t salt
    3-4 T oil

Method:

1. Heat 2 T oil in a teflon pan; sauté half of the onion. Add egg, stir-frying until egg becomes almost solid, then remove to a dish.

2. Add 1 T oil. Sauté onion. Add tomato wedges, salt and pepper. Stir and cook for 1 minute.

3. Add cooked eggs; stir and mix well. Serve hot.

Makes 4-6 servings.
Time: 15 minutes

Calories: 778   Carbohydrates: 19 gm
Protein: 28 gm   Fat: 66 gm

炒蛋

ONION SCRAMBLED EGGS
(Chao Dan)

Ingredients:

    6   large eggs
    1   t salt
    3   T oil
  2-4   green onions, minced

Method:

1. Beat eggs with salt. Add minced onions and mix well.
2. Heat oil in a teflon pan. Add eggs; stir and turn until they become solid. Remove to a serving dish. Serve hot.

Makes 6 servings
Time: 10 minutes

Calories: 862   Carbohydrates: 2 gm
Protein: 36 gm   Fat: 78 gm

蛋餃

EGG DUMPLINGS
(Dan Jiao)

Ingredients:

    ½   lb ground pork or beef
    ¼   C bamboo shoots or water chestnuts, minced
  3-4   dried mushrooms, soaked and minced
    ¼   onion, minced
   1½   t salt   (cont'd)

       1 t sherry
       1 t minced fresh ginger root
       ¼ t pepper
    1/8 t MSG (optional)
       5 eggs, well beaten
       ½ lb celery cabbage, cut into 2" sections
       4 T oil
       1 T soy sauce
       2 green onions, cut into 1" pieces
       ½ C water
       1 t sugar
          Pinch of pepper and MSG to taste

Method:

1. Blend the first nine ingredients thoroughly.
2. Heat 1 T oil in a teflon pan over medium heat. Add 1 T egg. When the egg is lightly cooked, quickly place 1 t meat on the left half of the omelet; fold over immediately to seal the edge of the omelet. Brown both sides and remove to a platter.
3. Add a few drops of oil and repeat the process until the eggs and filling are used up.
4. Spread celery cabbage evenly in the pan with the last five ingredients. Place egg dumplings on the vegetable; cover pan and cook for 10 minutes over medium heat. Serve hot.

Makes 8 servings
Time: 45 minutes

Calories: 1556   Carbohydrates: 17 gm
Protein: 72 gm   Fat: 132 gm

(Calculated with pork butt)

蛋捲

EGG OMELET AND BEEF ROLLS
(Dan Juan)

Ingredients:

    4 eggs, beaten
    ½ lb ground beef
    1 beef bouillon cube, softened in 1 T hot water
    2 T soy sauce
    1 T sherry
  1/8 t pepper
    2 green onions, minced
    1 t minced ginger root
    ½ t sugar
    ¼ C water chestnuts, coarsely minced
    1 t cornstarch
    2 T oil

Method:

1. Mix ground beef with the next nine ingredients; set aside.

2. Use a small piece of paper towel to spread a thin layer of oil in a teflon fry pan.

3. Heat pan over medium flame. Pour ⅓ of the beaten egg in the pan tipping it so that a layer of egg covers the bottom.

4. Cook until the surface of the egg dries. Remove and repeat the process (makes three egg omelets).

5. Spread ⅓ of the meat mixture evenly on one egg omelet and roll it up. Repeat to make three rolls.

6. Put 1 T oil in a teflon pan; put the rolls in. Cover and cook over low heat for 5 minutes.

7. Turn the rolls over; add 1 T oil, cover and cook over low heat for another 5-8 minutes.

8. Remove to a serving plate. Cut the rolls into ½" sections. Serve hot.

Makes 6 servings
Time: 40 minutes

Calories: 1268
Protein: 68 gm

Carbohydrates: 18 gm
Fat: 100 gm

EGG OMELET WITH PORK AND DRIED SHRIMP
(Xia Mi Dan Juan)

蝦米蛋捲

Ingredients:

- 4 eggs, beaten
- ½ lb ground pork butt
- 2 T dried shrimp (about 25 grams)
- 1 egg white
- 1 T soy sauce
- 1 T sherry
- 1/8 t pepper
- 2 green onions, minced
- 1 T minced ginger root
- 10 water chestnuts, chopped
- 2 T oil

Method:

1. Soak dried shrimp in hot water for 1 hour. Drain and mince.   (cont'd)

247

2. Thoroughly mix ground pork with the next eight ingredients.

3. Use a small piece of paper towel to spread a thin layer of oil on a teflon fry-pan.

4. Heat pan over medium heat. Pour ⅓ of the beaten egg in the pan, tipping it so that a thin layer of egg covers the bottom.

5. Cook until the surface of the egg dries. Remove and repeat the process (makes three omelet sheets).

6. Spread ⅓ of the meat mixture evenly on one egg omelet and roll it up. Repeat the process to make three rolls.

7. Put 1 T oil in the pan; add the rolls. Cover and cook over low heat for 5-8 minutes.

8. Turn the rolls, add 1 T oil. Cover and cook over low heat for another 5-8 minutes.

9. Remove to a serving plate; cut the rolls into ½" sections. Serve hot, plain or with sauce (see below).

Sauce:

    2 chicken bouillon cubes
 1½ C water
    1 T cornstarch blended with 2 T water

Soften the bouillon cubes in water and bring to a boil. Add cornstarch; stir and cook until the sauce thickens. Pour it on the egg omelets before serving.

Makes 6 servings
Time: 40 minutes

Calories: 1339   Carbohydrates: 21 gm
Protein: 86 gm   Fat: 98 gm

(Calculated with sauce)

HAM EGG FOO YOUNG
(Fu Rong Dan)

Ingredients:

    6 eggs, beaten
    2 oz ham, shredded
   ½ C shredded celery
    4 oz fresh mushrooms, shredded
    1 C bamboo shoots, shredded or 2 C fresh bean
        sprouts
   ¼ onion, shredded
    1 t salt
 1/8 t pepper
    1 t sherry
 1/8 t MSG (optional)
    4 T oil
    1 T minced green onion for garnishing

Method:

1. Gently mix all the ingredients together, except the oil, in a mixing bowl.

2. Heat 2 T oil in a teflon pan. Pour half of the egg mixture in the pan. Cook over medium heat until the surface of the egg is almost dry. Turn over and brown the other side, adding a few drops of oil if necessary.

3. Remove and fry the other portion in the same manner. Serve hot with sauce (next page) or without sauce.

Cooked shrimp, crab meat, roasted chicken meat, cooked pork etc. can be used in this dish.

Makes 6-8 servings
Time: 35 minutes

(cont'd)

Calories: 1197   Carbohydrates: 7 gm
Protein: 50 gm   Fat: 105 gm

Sauce:

    1½ C chicken broth
    2 T cornstarch

Mix the ingredients in a small sauce pan and bring to a boil, stirring constantly while cooking. Pour the sauce on the Egg Foo Young and sprinkle the minced onion on the sauce before serving.

Calories: 70   Carbohydrates: 14 gm
Protein: 2 gm   Fat: trace

TEA EGGS
(Cha Ye Dan)

Ingredients:

    1-2 doz eggs
    5 cloves
    5 whole star anise
    1 stick of cinnamon
    1-3 T soy sauce
    1-2 T salt
    5 black tea bags

Method:

1. Put eggs in a deep sauce pan. Fill pan with water until all the eggs are covered. Cook over medium heat for 30 minutes.

2. Plunge the eggs into cold water for a few minutes. Make cracks all over the shells (do not shell them).

3. Place the cracked eggs in a deep sauce pan. Cover eggs with water, add the rest of the ingredients and bring to a boil.

4. Cover and reduce to low heat; simmer for 30 minutes.

5. Let the cooked eggs stay in the covered pan of water for 3-4 hours (or in the refrigerator overnight).

Serve hot (by re-heating) or cold.

These eggs are especially good for picnics and are also good to serve as a snack, appetizers, hors d'oeuvres or part of a meal.

One egg:

Calories: 80	Carbohydrates: trace
Protein: 6 gm	Fat: 6 gm

Ingredients:

  1 dozen duck eggs or chicken eggs
  ½ lb salt
  1 qt water
  1 large glass jar or plastic container

Method:

1. Boil water and add salt. Stir until salt is dissolved completely.

2. When the salted water is cold, transfer it into the jar or plastic container.

3. Gently put the eggs in the salted water. Let them stay in the water for 3-4 weeks.

4. Hard boil the eggs before serving.

Serve with rice or rice porridge for breakfast.

Pickled eggs can be cooked with other ingredients. (See recipes on pages 253 and 255).

Fresh eggs can be put into the salted water from time to time. Mark the date on the shells before putting them in.

1 large hen egg:

Calories: 80   Carbohydrates: trace
Protein: 6 gm   Fat: 6 gm

STEAMED MEAT WITH PICKLED EGGS
(Xian Dan Zheng Rou)

醃蛋蒸肉

Ingredients:

- 3 pickled eggs (see recipe for making the pickled eggs, page 252)
- 2 lb. ground pork
- 3-4 medium size dried mushrooms, soaked and diced
- 3-4 T dried shrimp, soaked and minced (about 50 grams)
- ½ C water chestnuts, coarsely minced
- 2 T minced onion
- 1 T sherry
- 1 T minced ginger root
- ½ T soy sauce
- ¼ t pepper
- 2 t sesame oil

Method:

1. Mix all the ingredients together except pickled eggs. Put the mixed meat in a heat-proof bowl; press flat on the top.
2. Crack the eggs (unbeaten) one by one on the meat.
3. Steam for 40 minutes.
4. Serve hot.

The left-overs can be re-heated in a steamer or in a pan. They can also be cut into small pieces and cooked with soup.

Makes 6-8 servings
Time: 45 minutes

Calories: 2806   Carbohydrates: 10 gm
Protein: 207 gm   Fat: 215 gm

Ingredients:

6 dozen duck eggs
Soil or mud
Rice husk or broken straw

For the Solution:
5000 cc water
75 gm black tea, any brand
250 gm wood ash
750 gm lime
250 gm salt
150 gm NaOH
Mix all the above ingredients together in a large earthenware or plastic container to make the solution base.

Method:

1. Wear a pair of rubber gloves. Gently drop duck eggs in the solution.
2. Soak the eggs in the solution for 4 weeks. Turn once every week, always wearing rubber gloves.
3. Remove the eggs from the solution at the end of fourth week.
4. Mix soil with water to form a thick, mud-like paste.
5. Coat each egg with a layer of mud-paste (⅓" thick). Coat with a layer of dry husk on the mud, then wrap in a plastic bag.
6. Keep the mud-coated eggs in a dry place for one week. They are then ready to use.

These eggs can be stored at room temperature for as long as
2 to 3 months.

Thanks to Mrs. T. S. Chen for this recipe.

SAN HUANG DAN
(San Huang Dan)

Ingredients:

  2 Thousand Years' eggs (page 254)
  2 pickled eggs (page 252)
  2 eggs
 2-3 T oil
   Pinch of pepper and onion powder to taste

Method:

1. Gently crack and wash the mud away from the Thousand
Years' eggs. Shell and cut the eggs into ½" cubes. Set aside.

2. Break the pickled eggs in a bowl. Place the pickled egg
yolks in a small dish and cut them into small pieces.

3. Break eggs into the pickled egg whites and beat together
for 2 minutes.

4. Heat oil in a teflon pan. Stir-fry pickled egg yolks and
Thousand Year's eggs together for 1 minute.

5. Add beaten eggs; stir and mix until they become solid.
Serve hot.

Thousand Years' eggs and pickled eggs can be purchased
in Oriental stores.

Makes 6 servings
Time: 10 minutes

**THOUSAND-YEARS' EGGS
WITH SOY SAUCE**
(Jiang You Pi Dan)

Ingredients:

3 Thousand Years' eggs, from an Oriental grocery
store or home-made (see recipe on page 254)
1 t sesame oil
1 T soy sauce

Method:

1. Gently crack the mud away from the eggs; wash and
shell them.
2. Cut the eggs into quarters; arrange on a serving plate.
3. Mix soy sauce and sesame oil; pour the mixture on egg
pieces.
Serve as appetizers, hors d'oeuvres or with rice porridge,
or rice.

desserts and snacks (dim-sum)

DIM - SUM

Recently Chinese Dim-Sum has gained popularity in the United States. Dim-Sum is a broad name for many dishes that could be served as brunch, lunch, snack, appetizer, hors d' oeuvres or dessert. Many of these Dim-Sum dishes are nutritious, tasty and balanced meals by themselves. In addition to these recipes included in this section, there are many others in different sections of the book that could be served as Dim-Sum.

Here are the recipes:

Bean thread and meat ball soup (p. 31)
Noodle soup with assorted vegetables (p.32)
Wonton soup (p.34)
Dried beef slices (p.57)
Steamed meat in noodle case (p.64)
Pearl meat balls (p.69)
Sweet sour meat balls (p.70)
Sweet sour spareribs (p.80)
Barbecued spareribs (p.81)
Red broiled pork (p.86)
Salted cold chicken (p.102)
Wined chicken (p.104)
Smoked chicken (p.107)
Sauteed chicken wing (p.117)
Barbecued chicken wings (p.118)
Smoked fish (p. 136)
Phoenix tailed shrimp (p. 148)
Shrimp toast (p. 150)
Shrimp balls (p. 151)
Baby cucumber Szechwan style (p.173)
Braised mushrooms (p.175)
Pickled spicy vegetables (p.182)
Braised wheat gluten (p.188)
Spiced dry bean curd (p.198)
Chicken rice (p.222)
Rice with crab or lobster meat (p.223)
Shrimp rice (p. 224)
Sausage rice (p.225)

(cont'd)

Red broiled pork rice (p. 226)
Curried beef rice (p.227)
Fried rice with assorted vegetables and ham (p.228)
Eighth of twelve month rice chowder (p.230)
Cold noodles (p.234)
Fried noodles (chow mein) soft type (p.235)
Fried noodles (chow mein) crisp type (p.237)
Tea eggs (p.250)
Thousand-years' eggs with soy sauce (p.256)

CHINESE TEA
(Qing Cha)

清茶

Ingredients:

    1 heaping tablespoonful of your favorite tea leaves
    6 cups of boiling water

Method:

    1. Put the tea leaves in a tea pot.
    2. Pour the vigorously boiling water into the tea pot.
    3. Cover the tea pot. Let the tea leaves steep for 3-5 minutes. Stir the tea leaves with a spoon for even flavor before serving.
    Serve hot without sugar or cream.

SESAME SEED CANDY
(Zi Ma Tang)

Ingredients:

    2 T oil
    ¾ C granulated sugar
    1 C sesame seeds, about ¼ pound

Method:

1. Heavily grease a cookie sheet and a rolling pin (using any kind of shortening). Set aside.

2. Heat oil in a small pan. Add sugar; stir and cook over medium heat until sugar is completely melted (the color of the melted sugar will be light brown but not burned).

3. Remove from heat; add the sesame seeds immediately to the sugar and mix quickly.

4. Pour on to the greased sheet and wait for 1 minute then roll out into a 1/8" thick sheet. It will be very sticky to roll.

5. Cut into desired shape (square, rectangle, triangle, etc.) while it is lukewarm.

6. Break into pieces when it is cold.

A friend of mine suggested using a teflon cookie sheet and rolling pin to prevent sticking.

Calories: 1466   Carbohydrates 173 gm
Protein: 21 gm   Fat: 83 gm

WALNUT CANDIES
(Hu Tao Tang)

胡桃糖

Ingredients:

    ½ lb walnuts
    ½ lb granulated sugar
    ½ C powdered sugar
  1½ C oil for deep-frying
       Water

Method:

1. Boil 5-6 cups of water in a sauce pan; turn off the heat and put the walnuts in the hot water for 5 minutes. Drain. Repeat the process three times.

2. Dissolve the granulated sugar in 2 cups of water. Put the drained walnuts in the sugared water and store overnight in a container in the refrigerator. Turn them from time to time.

3. Drain and dry the walnuts on a rack for four hours.

4. Heat oil in a wok or in a sauce pan over high heat; deep-fry the walnuts until golden brown.

5. Arrange the fried walnuts in a dish and sprinkle with powdered sugar while they are hot. Serve hot or cold.

Calories of the following ingredients:

½ lb granulated sugar: 873
½ C powdered sugar: 230
½ lb walnuts: 1476

杏仁豆腐

ALMOND BEAN CURD
(Xing Ren Dou Fu)

Ingredients:

- 1 T unflavored gelatin (one envelope)
- 1¾ C milk
- ½ C sugar
- 1 T almond extract
- 1 C fruit cocktail, mandarin orange segments, lychees, or pineapple tidbits, fresh or canned

Method:

1. Mix gelatin with sugar
2. Add sugar mixture to 1 C boiling milk. Stir until gelatin is completely dissolved.
3. Add ¾ C cold milk and almond extract.
4. Pour the gelatin into a square mold. Chill in the refrigerator until firm.
5. Cut the gelatin into small squares (about ½" cubes). Serve with the chilled fruits and their juices.

Makes 6 servings

Calories: 885
Protein: 22 gm

Carbohydrates: 150 gm
Fat: 16 gm

(Calculated with 1 C fruit cocktail)

WALNUT SOUP DESSERT
(Hu Tao Tian Tang)

Ingredients:

1 C walnuts
¾ C sugar
¼ t salt
2 C water
2 T cornstarch blended in ½ C water
Water

Method:

1. Boil 5 cups of water in a sauce pan; turn off heat and put the walnuts in the hot water for 1 minute. Drain. Repeat process three times.

2. Put the drained walnuts and 2 C water in a blender; blend for 2 minutes.

3. Pour the blended walnuts in a sauce pan, add sugar and salt and bring to boil. Stir while cooking.

4. Add blended cornstarch and cook until the soup thickens. Serve hot.

Makes 6 servings
Time: 25 minutes

Calories: 1427   Carbohydrates: 182 gm
Protein: 26 gm   Fat: 75 gm

貂皮香蕉

BANANA IN MINK COAT
(Diao Pi Xiang Jiao)

Ingredients:

½ C black sesame seeds (about 1/8 lb)
½ C powdered sugar
4 medium size bananas
1 egg
⅓ C cornstarch
⅓ C flour plus ½ t baking powder
¼ C cold water
2 T sugar
¼ C flour for coating
1 C oil for deep-frying

Method:

1. Roast sesame seeds in an oven at 300° for 12 minutes.

2. When sesame seeds cool, mix with powdered sugar and blend in a blender into a fine powder. Set aside.

3. Peel bananas and slice crosswise into ¾" long pieces. Coat the banana pieces with a thin layer of flour.

4. Mix cornstarch, flour, baking powder, egg, water and sugar together to make a batter.

5. Heat oil in a sauce pan or wok. Dip the flour-coated banana pieces in the batter one by one and fry until golden brown. Remove from the oil and put on a platter.

6. Serve the fried bananas along with a dish of sesame-seed powder.

7. Coat the banana pieces with a layer of sesame-seed powder by rolling the banana pieces in the powder before eating.

Sesame powder (steps 1 and 2 of the "Method") can be prepared in advance and kept for weeks.

Makes 6 servings
Time: 25 minutes

Calories: 1760   Carbohydrates: 286 gm
Protein: 27 gm   Fat: 61 gm

(Calculated with 2 T oil for deep-frying.)

WHITE (SILVER) WOOD EAR SOUP DESSERT
(Pai Mu Er Tang)

Ingredients:

    1 oz white (silver) wood ears
    1 C mandarin orange segements or your favorite
       fruits
    2 C water
    ½ C sugar

Method:

1. Soak the wood ears in hot water for 10 minutes. Wash and drain.
2. Put the water and sugar in a sauce pan; bring to a boil. Add wood ears and cook for 5 minutes.
3. Add fruit and mix well. Serve hot or cold.

Makes 6 servings
Time: 20 minutes

(See page 20)

Ingredients:

- ½ C rice
- ½ C black sesame seeds (about 1/8 lb)
- 4 C water
- ¾ C sugar, or to taste
- 2 T roasted sunflower seeds or slivered almond for garnishing
- ¼ t salt

Method:

1. Soak rice in water for 2 hours. Rinse and drain.
2. Roast sesame seeds in a 300° oven for 12 minutes.
3. Blend rice, sesame seeds and water in a blender for 2-3 minutes.
4. Pour the blended rice mixture into a sauce pan; cook over medium heat for 10 minutes. Stir while cooking.
5. Add sugar; stir and cook for 3 minutes more. Garnish with sunflower seeds or slivered almond before serving. Serve hot or cold.

Makes 6-8 servings
Time: 30 minutes

Calories: 1231   Carbohydrates: 235 gm
Protein: 16 gm   Fat: 28 gm

(Garnishing is not included)

EIGHT TREASURES RICE PUDDING
(Ba Bao Fan)

Ingredients:

1 lb glutinous rice (sweet rice) cooked, (boiled or
  steamed), —cooking instructions are given
  in this recipe
4 T sugar
1 recipe of red bean paste, (see recipe on page 269)
  or canned bean paste sold in Oriental
  grocery stores
  Several kinds of preserved fruits and nuts for
  garnishing. For example: fruit and peel mix,
  raisins, dried plums, dried dates, candied lotus
  seeds, walnuts, shelled watermelon seeds, shelled
  pumpkin seeds, candied cherries and
  candied apricots.

Method:

1. Mix rice with sugar.
2. Heavily grease a 7" bowl with shortening.
3. Arrange the dried fruits and nuts on the greased bowl in several circles with the red color in the center and surrounded by alternate rows of dark and light colors.
4. Divide the rice into four portions. Place one portion over fruit and nut arrangement to form a concave layer.
5. Add bean paste on the rice layer and cover the bean paste with the other portion of the rice. Repeat the process to make two puddings.
6. Steam the rice pudding for 40 minutes. Turn the bowl upside down on a large platter. Pour hot sauce over the pudding before serving.   *(cont'd)*

267

Makes 10 servings

One pudding:

Calories: 2030   Carbohydrates: 381 gm
Protein: 37 gm   Fat: 40 gm

Sauce:

Mix together 2 t cornstarch, 2 T sugar and ½ C water;
bring to a boil. Stir while cooking. Pour over the rice pudding before serving.

The nutrition information for the sauce:

Calories: 100   Carbohydrates: 26 gm
Protein: 0   Fat: 0

Boiled Glutinous Rice:

Put 1 lb glutinous rice and 3½ C water in a small sauce
pan; bring to a boil. Uncover and continue boiling the rice
over medium heat until water has evaporated. Cover pan
tightly; turn to lowest heat and simmer for 20 minutes.

Steamed Glutinous Rice:

Soak 1 lb of glutinous rice in water for 2 hours. Drain. Put a
layer of cheese cloth in a tier of a steamer; steam for 1 hour.

The cooked rice, boiled or steamed, is enough to make two
rice puddings.

The rice pudding (steps 2-5 of the "Method") can be frozen
for months before being steamed. Before serving, thaw and
steam for 40 minutes. You could make several puddings at the
same time.

RED BEAN PASTE
(Dou Sha)

Ingredients:

    ½ lb Chinese red beans or kidney beans
    ½ lb dark brown sugar
    ⅓ C vegetable oil or lard
    ½ t salt
    4 C or more of water

Method:

1. Cook beans with water in a pressure cooker for 30 minutes or in regular pan until tender. Pour off excess water and let the beans cool.

2. Blend the cold, cooked beans in a blender into a smooth paste.

3. Heat oil or lard in a sauce pan (a non-stick pan is preferable), add bean paste, brown sugar and salt; stir and mix for 20-25 minutes over medium heat.

4. Chill the bean paste before using.

This bean paste is the basic ingredient for several recipes in this book. (See pages 267, 272, and 274).

This recipe is enough to make two Eight Treasures Rice Puddings (7" bowl) on page 267.

The bean paste can be frozen for 4-6 months.

Calories: 2262   Carbohydrates: 357 gm
Protein: 50 gm   Fat: 76 gm

杏仁餅干

ALMOND COOKIES
(Xing Ren Bing Gan)

Ingredients:

- 2 C all purpose flour
- ¾ - 1 C sugar
- 1 t soda
- ¼ t baking powder
- ¼ t salt
- 1 egg
- 1 T almond extract
- 1 C vegetable oil or lard
- 36 blanched almonds (optional)
- 1-2 drops of yellow coloring

Method:

1. Put sugar, oil (or lard), salt, egg, almond extract, food coloring, soda, and baking powder in a mixing bowl. Mix with an electric mixer until smooth.

2. Add flour and mix with your hands to form a soft dough.

3. Form the dough into balls about 1" in diameter and place an inch apart on a greased cookie sheet.

4. Gently press an almond in the center of each ball.

5. Bake 15 minutes in a preheated 350° oven. Makes 3 dozen cookies.

Brushing the cookies with beaten egg before adding the almond will give the cookies a shiny appearance after baking.

Calories: 3442
Protein: 30 gm

Carbohydrates: 325 gm
Fat: 228 gm

(Approximately 96 calories per cookie)

270

STEAMED CAKE
(Zheng Dan Gao)

Ingredients:

    1½ C all purpose flour
     3 eggs
     ½ C milk
     1 C brown sugar
     1 t baking powder
     ½ t baking soda
     ½ C oil or lard
     1 t vanilla
     ¼ t salt

Method:

1. Beat eggs, milk, oil, vanilla, salt and sugar in mixing bowl until smooth.

2. Add flour, baking powder and soda. Mix well.

3. Pour the batter in a greased bowl or baking pan. Steam in a covered, boiling steamer for 45 minutes. Remove the steamed cake to a plate. Serve warm or cold.

Do not open the lid while steaming!

Makes 12-20 pieces
Time: 50 minutes

Calories: 2743
Protein: 41 gm

Carbohydrates: 350 gm
Fat: 134 gm

豆沙煎餅

BEAN PASTE PAN CAKE
(Dou Sha Jian Bing)

Ingredients:

        3 large eggs
        1 C flour
        3 T sugar
        ⅔ C water
        ½ recipe of bean paste on page 269 or canned
           bean paste sold in Oriental grocery stores
        5 T oil

Method:

1. Blend the first 4 ingredients in a mixing bowl into a smooth paste.

2. Brush a non-stick pan with a thin layer of oil; pour ¼ of batter into the pan, tipping the pan so that a thin layer of the batter covers the pan. Turn to low heat and cook until the surface dries. Remove and repeat the process to make 4 pan cakes.

3. Place ¼ of the bean paste in the center of a pan cake. Flatten the bean paste into a 2" square. Fold the 4 sides of the pan cake on top of the bean paste and press (the edges of the pan cake can be over-lapped). Repeat with remaining pan cakes.

4. Heat the oil in a non-stick pan; add the folded pan cakes and fry over medium heat until both sides are golden brown. Cut into slices before serving. Serve hot.

Makes 6-8 servings
Time: 30 minutes

Calories: 1906　　　　　Carbohydrates: 307 gm
Protein: 55 gm　　　　　Fat: 57 gm

HOME-MADE DONUTS
(You Zha Bing)

Ingredients:

    1 tube (8 oz) ready-to-bake, home-style
       chilled biscuits
       Oil for deep-frying
       Powdered sugar for coating

Method:

1. Open the tube. Punch a 1½" hole in the middle of each biscuit.

2. Heat oil; fry the biscuits until brown.

3. Put the powdered sugar in a plastic bag. Put the fried biscuits in the bag and shake until each is coated with sugar.

This is not a Chinese food. I learned it from a cashier lady in a supermarket. She told me that she made donuts from the biscuits and that they were very good and economical. I tried her recipe and was very successful so I would like to share it with my readers. I add powdered cinnamon to the sugar when I want cinnamon flavored donuts.

Makes 10 donuts　(108 calories in each donut.)

Calories: 1087　　　　　Carbohydrates: 149 gm
Protein: 15 gm　　　　　Fat: 51 gm

(Calculated with 3 T oil for deep-frying.)

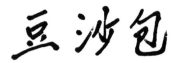
Ingredients:

½ recipe Chinese bread dough
(see recipe on page 238)
½ recipe red bean paste (see page 269)
½ C chopped walnuts (optional)
12 2" square wax paper

Method:

1. Roast walnuts in pre-heated oven at 300° for 12 minutes. Add to the red bean paste and mix well.
2. Follow the Chinese bread recipe until second rising, then divide the dough into 12 pieces.
3. Flatten each of the pieces of dough with the palm of your hand, then roll into 4" round wrappers. The center of the wrapper should be thicker than the edges.
4. Put 1 tablespoon of bean paste in the center of each wrapper. Pinch pleats around the edges of the wrapper. Gather all the pleats on the top and twist to seal.

5. Put each stuffed sweet bun on a piece of wax paper. Arrange the buns 1" apart in a tier of a steamer. Steam over

boiling water for 15 minutes. Do not open the lid while steaming. Serve hot as a snack or as a dessert.

Cold sweet buns can be re-steamed for 5 minutes before serving.

Calories: 2562   Carbohydrates: 433 gm
Protein: 56 gm   Fat: 68 gm

(The walnuts are not included in this calculation.)

MEAT STUFFED STEAMED BUNS
(Pao Zi)

Ingredients:

    1 lb ground pork or beef
    1 box (10 oz) quick-frozen chopped spinach or
      mustard greens
    2 T soy sauce
  ½ t salt
1/8 t pepper
    1 onion, chopped
    1 T sesame oil
    2 t minced ginger root
    1 tube (12 oz), 15 ready-to-bake home-style
      chilled biscuits

Method:

1. Mix the first eight ingredients together thoroughly. This mixture will be the filling.

2. Open the biscuit tube. Put the biscuits on a floured board. *(cont'd)*

3. Flatten each biscuit with hand then roll into 3" round wrapper. The center of the wrapper should be thicker than the edges.

4. Put 1 tablespoon of filling in the center of the wrapper. Pinch pleats near the edges of the wrapper. Gather all the pleats on the top center and twist.

5. Put each stuffed meat bun on a piece of wax paper (the wax paper will be slightly larger than the bun). Arrange the buns 1 inch apart in a tier of a steamer. Steam over boiling water for 15 minutes. Do not open the lid while steaming! Serve hot as lunch, snacks or dinner with soup.

Stuffed meat buns can be prepared in advance. Re-heat the buns in a tier of a steamer over boiling water for 8 minutes before serving.

Steamed meat buns can be frozen. Thaw and re-steam for 5 minutes before serving.

Makes 15 meat stuffed buns.

Calories: 2333   Carbohydrates: 171 gm
Protein: 112 gm   Fat: 127 gm

(Calculated with ground pork butt.)

生煎包

MEAT STUFFED PAN-FRIED BUNS
(Sun Jian Pao)

1. Spread 2 T oil in a non-stick frying pan; arrange the wrapped meat-stuffed buns (uncooked) in the pan. Add ⅔ C of water; cover pan and bring to a boil. Reduce to medium heat and cook until water dries and a layer of light brown crust forms on the bottom of the buns. Serve hot.

Calories: 2583   Carbohydrates: 171 gm
Protein: 112 gm   Fat: 155 gm

RED BROILED PORK STUFFED BUNS
(Cha Shao Pao)

Ingredients:

½ recipe Chinese steamed bread dough (recipe on page 238)
¼ recipe thinly sliced pork (recipe on page 86)
4 green onions, shredded
1 T shredded ginger root
1 T oil
1 T water
3 T Hoisin sauce

Method:

1. Mix the last six ingredients together thoroughly. Use this mixture as the filling for the buns.

2. Divide the dough into 10 round balls.

3. Flatten each piece of small dough with the palm of your hand on a floured board. Roll the dough out into a 3½" round wrapper. The center of the wrapper should be thicker than the edges.

4. Put 1 heaping tablespoon of filling in the center of the wrapper. Gather all the edges together at the top; pinch the edges together and twist to make sure they are sealed.

5. Put each stuffed bun on a 2" square of wax paper. Arrange them in a tier of a steamer (1" apart). Steam over boiling water for 15 minutes. Do not open the lid while steaming! Serve hot as lunch, a snack or part of a meal.

Cold buns can be re-steamed for 5-8 minutes before being served again. They can also be frozen.

Makes 10 buns

Calories: 2148
Protein: 70 gm

Carbohydrates: 260 gm
Fat: 90 gm

(See page 20)

MEAT DUMPLINGS
(Jiao Zi)

Ingredients and methods for filling:

You could choose any one of the following three fillings.

I.

 1 lb ground pork or beef
10 oz chopped frozen vegetables (spinach, mustard greens, turnip greens, etc.) thawed and squeeze dried
 2 green onions, minced
 1 T minced ginger root
 3 T soy sauce
¼ t salt
¼ t pepper
 1 T sesame oil
1/8 t MSG (optional)

Mix all the ingredients together thoroughly.

Nutrition information for this filling:

Calories: 1444
Protein: 93 gm

Carbohydrates: 17 gm
Fat: 111 gm

(Calculated with ground pork butt.)

II.

    ½ lb ground pork
    ½ lb frozen or fresh shelled shrimp, minced
    1 C fresh celery cabbage, chopped and squeeze dried
    3 medium size dried mushrooms, soaked and minced
    1 T minced ginger root
    3 T soy sauce
    ¼ t salt
    ¼ t white pepper
    1 t sesame oil
    ¼ onion, minced
  1/8 t MSG

Mix all the ingredients together thoroughly.

Nutrition information for this filling:

Calories: 895   Carbohydrates: 8 gm
Protein: 86 gm   Fat: 54 gm

III.

    ½ lb fresh or frozen shelled shrimp, minced
    ¼ lb ground pork
    ½ C minced bamboo shoots
    4 medium size dried mushrooms, soaked and minced
    ¼ onion, minced
    1 T minced ginger root
    3 T soy sauce
    ¼ t salt
    ¼ t white pepper
    1 t sesame oil
  1/8 t MSG (optional)

Mix all the ingredients together thoroughly.

Nutrition information for this filling:

Calories: 625 Carbohydrates: 19 gm
Protein: 68 gm Fat: 30 gm

Ingredients for the wrapper:

2½ C all purpose flour
1 C cold water

Method for the wrapper:

1. Mix flour and water in a mixing bowl to form a dough.
2. Knead the dough on a floured board for 5 minutes.
3. Return the kneaded dough in the mixing bowl; cover with a dampened cloth. Let it stand for 3 hours.
4. Remove dough to a floured board; knead again until very smooth.
5. Form the dough into a cylinder about 1" in diameter.
6. Cut the cylindrical roll, evenly, into ½" thick pieces.
7. Flatten each piece with the palm of your hand and roll out into 2½" round thin wrapper. The center of the wrapper should be thicker than the edges.

The nutrition information of this wrapper:

Calories: 1050   Carbohydrates: 220 gm
Protein: 30 gm   Fat: 3 gm

Method for wrapping:

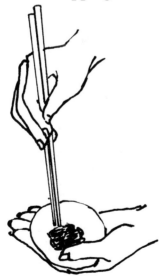

1. Place 1 teaspoon of filling in the center of a dumpling wrapper.

2. Fold the wrapper in half across the filling and pinch once in the center.

3. Make 3 or 4 pleats on one side of the center and then the other, shaping the dumpling into a 3 sided, crescent shape.

4. Pinch the edges along the pleated side in order to seal tightly.

Method for cooking:

There are three ways to cook the dumplings. You may choose any one of them.

I. BOILED DUMPLINGS
(Shui Jiao)

1. Fill a large deep sauce pan one third full of water. Bring to a boil.

2. Drop 20 dumplings carefully into the boiling water; stir gently with the back of a wooden spoon to prevent the dumplings from sticking to each other and to the bottom of the pan.

3. Cover pan and bring to a boil. Add ⅔ C cold water, cover pan and bring to a boil again. Add ⅔ C cold water, cover pan and bring to a boil once more. (This prevents the dumplings from breaking apart in the rapidly boiling water.)

4. Remove the cooked dumplings with a slotted spoon. Repeat the process until all the dumplings are cooked. Serve hot (see "to serve").

II. FRIED DUMPLINGS (Pan Stickers)
(Quo Tie)

1. Spread 2 T oil in a 10" teflon fry pan; arrange enough dumplings in the pan to cover the bottom, without overlapping.
2. Add ⅔ C cold water; cover pan and bring to a boil.
3. Turn to medium heat until water has evaporated.
4. Add 1 T oil and fry for ½ minute more. Remove the dumplings to a platter by turning them upside down on the platter. Serve hot (see "to serve").

III. STEAMED DUMPLINGS
(Zheng Jiao)

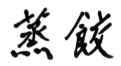

1. Lightly grease cheese cloth on a tier of a steamer.
2. Arrange the dumplings neatly on the greased tier.
3. Cover and steam over boiling water for 12 minutes.
4. Remove the steamed dumplings to a platter. Serve hot (see "to serve").

For dipping:

>   Soy sauce
>   Vinegar
>   Hot sauce or hot oil
>   Mashed garlic with soy sauce

Have the above ingredients ready and put them in separate small bowls. You may prepare them a few hours ahead. Cover with foil and keep them in the refrigerator.

To serve:

Set the large platter of cooked dumplings in the center of the dinner table along with the small bowls of dips. Dip the dumplings before eating.

Serve dumplings as a snack or as a complete meal.

The wrapped dumplings can be kept in the freezer for weeks before cooking.

To freeze the uncooked dumplings: Arrange the dumplings on a tray (uncovered) and keep them in the freezer overnight. Place the frozen dumplings in a plastic bag, seal well and keep frozen. The dumplings do not need to be thawed before cooking.

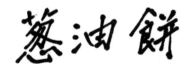

GREEN ONION CRISP PANCAKE
(Cong You Bing)

Ingredients:

    2-4 green onions, minced
      1 t salt
      1 C boiling water
      2 C flour
      2 T oil

Method:

1. Mix minced onion with salt. Set aside.

2. Pour boiling water slowly into the flour in a mixing bowl. Mix water and flour with a wooden spoon or a pair of chopsticks.

3. Knead the dough until smooth on a floured board.

4. Divide dough into 4 equal pieces. Roll each piece of dough out into 6-8" round sheets.

5. Brush a layer of oil on the sheets and sprinkle a layer of onion on the oil-brushed sheets.

6. Roll up the dough jelly roll style. Form the roll into a round snail shape, then press down and roll out ½-¼" thick.

7. Heat about 2 T oil in a skillet over medium heat. Place the cakes in the pan and cook for 2 minutes with the lid on. Turn and fry until brown and crisp.

8. Cut into quarters. Serve hot.

These cakes can be served as a snack or at dinner in place of bread or rice.

These cakes can be cooked in advance. Before serving, reheat in a preheated oven at 300° for a few minutes.

Makes 6 servings
Time: 25 minutes

Calories: 1097
Protein: 24 gm

Carbohydrates: 179 gm
Fat: 30 gm

春捲皮

SPRING ROLL AND WONTON SKIN
(Zhun Juan Pi)

Ingredients:

  2 C flour
  1 large egg
  ½ C cold water
  ¼ C cornstarch for flouring board

Method:

1. Mix the first three ingredients in a large mixing bowl to make a dough. Knead the dough on a floured board until smooth (about 15 minutes).

2. Return the kneaded dough to the mixing bowl. Cover the bowl with a damp cloth and let it stand for 30 minutes.

3. Place the dough on the floured board; knead for 5 minutes.

4. Roll the dough out with a rolling pin again and again. Flour the dough from time to time to prevent stickiness.

5. When the dough becomes very thin, cut it into 6" squares for spring roll skins or cut into 3" squares for Wonton skins.

Makes about one pound Spring Roll or Wonton skins.

Calories: 920   Carbohydrates: 176 gm
Protein: 30 gm   Fat: 8 gm

Both ready-made skins from the stores or home-made skins for spring rolls and Wontons can be frozen when wrapped in a well sealed plastic bag. Thaw before using.

When the skins are stored in the freezer too long, the edges of the skins will be dried and slightly brittle. The skins can be

286

revived by putting a dampened paper napkin in the package with the skins, then place the whole thing in a well sealed plastic bag. Keep the bag in the refrigerator for one or two days. The skins will be revived as fresh ones.

FRIED WONTON
(Zha Hun Dun)

Ingredients:

    ½ lb ground beef
    ½ C water chestnuts, minced
    2 oz fresh mushrooms, minced or 2-3 dried
       mushrooms, soaked and minced
    ¼ onion, minced
    1 t sherry
    1 t minced ginger root
    ¼ t pepper
1/8 t MSG (optional)
    1 t salt
    1 lb Wonton skin, about 70 to 80 pieces
       Oil for deep-frying

Method:

1. Mix the first nine ingredients thoroughly. This will be used as Wonton filling.

2. Put ½ t of the filling in the center of the skin. Fold it up to make a Wonton. See the sketches on page 289.

3. Heat oil to 400°. Fry a few Wontons at a time until golden brown. Serve hot.

Serve Fried Wonton hot with vinegar, mustard sauce, sweet and sour sauce or diluted Hoisin sauce. See below.

Wonton skin may be purchased from Oriental grocery stores or may be home-made. The recipe for the Wonton skins is on page 286.

Fried Wontons can be prepared in advance and frozen. Before serving, reheat in a pre-heated oven at 300° for 5 to 8 minutes or until they are completely heated.

To freeze the wrapped Wontons: arrange the Wontons on a tray and keep in the freezer, uncovered, over night. Carefully place the frozen Wontons in a plastic bag and seal well. The frozen Wontons can be kept for three months in the freezer. Frozen Wontons can be fried without thawing.

Makes 70-80 wontons

Calories: 1583	Carbohydrates: 188 gm
Protein: 73 gm	Fat: 56 gm

(Deep-fry oil is not included in this calculation).

Sweet and Sour Sauce:

Bring to a boil a mixture of the following ingredients:
4 T sugar
4 T catsup
4 T vinegar
4 T water
2 t cornstarch

Serve cold.

Nutrition information for the Sweet and Sour Sauce:

Calories: 241	Carbohydrates: 68 gm
Protein: 0	Fat: 0

Mustard Sauce:

Mix the following ingredients into a smooth paste:

 2 T mustard powder
 2 T cold water
 ½ t vinegar
 1/8 t salt

Refrigerate before using.

To Fold Wontons:

1. Put ½ teaspoon of filling in the center of a Wonton skin (wrapper).

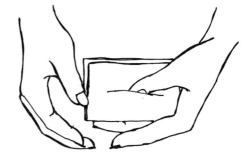

2. Fold the wrapper in half toward you (with the filling in the center).

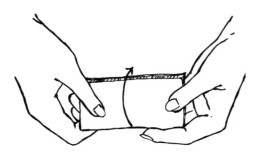

3. Fold the wrapper in half once more in the same direction.

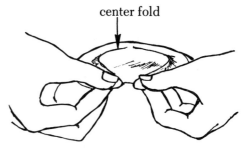

center fold

4. Holding the corners at the center fold, pull forward.

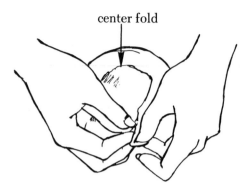

center fold

5. Overlap the corners of the center fold, moisten and press to seal.

6. Wontons should have the appearance of little nurse's caps.

SPRING ROLLS (EGG ROLLS)
(Zhun Juan)

Ingredients:

½ lb ground beef or pork
3 T soy sauce
1 T sherry
¼ t pepper
1 T minced fresh ginger root
½ t brown sugar
2 T cornstarch
1/8 t MSG
1 C onion, shredded
1 C celery or bamboo shoots, shredded, or
   1 C fresh bean sprouts
½ lb cabbage, shredded
¼ lb fresh mushrooms, shredded
4 T oil

1 lb spring roll skins, about 20 pieces
(You can buy the ready made ones in an Oriental
grocery store or make them at home. The recipe
is on page 286)
Mix 1 T flour and ½ C water together for sealing.
Oil for deep-frying

Method:

I. Filling

1. Mix beef with 2 T soy sauce and the next six ingredients.
2. Heat 4 T oil in a teflon pan. Add beef and stir-fry until color turns and the pieces are separated.
3. Add onion; stir with the beef for 2 minutes.
4. Add celery, cabbage, mushrooms and 1 T soy sauce; stir and cook until the cabbage is half done (just mix with the meat, the vegetables are still raw). Set aside and let it cool.

II. Wrapping

A. Old way:

1. Place 1 heaping tablespoonful of cold filling diagonally across the upper part (nearest you) of the wrapper.
2. Shape the filling into a 4" long x 1" wide rectangle.
3. Fold the upper triangular flap over the filling; press and roll once.
4. Fold both flaps from the left and right sides on top of the enclosed filling.
5. Brush the edges of the open triangular flap with a thin layer of sealing.
6. Roll it up until the edges of the sealing-brushed triangular flap seals the whole roll.

Be sure to wrap and seal the spring rolls well. If not, the spring rolls either will burst while frying, or a large quantity of oil will get into the filling and make the spring rolls very greasy.

B. New way:

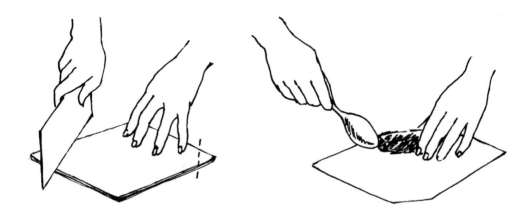

1. With about one pound of Spring Roll skins (wrappers) on a cutting board, trim corners (about 1") off two opposite sides.

2. With a trimmed corner nearest you, place a heaping T of cold filling across the upper part of a wrapper.

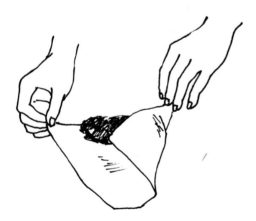

3. Fold both flaps from the left and right sides over the filling.

4. Roll the folded Spring Roll up to within about 3" of the end.

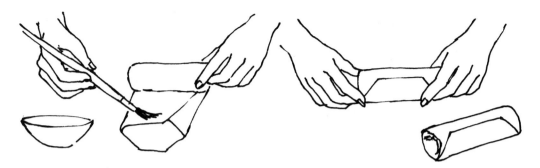

5. Brush the folded flaps of the wrapper with a thin layer of sealing.

6. Finish rolling, making sure the sealing-brushed flaps and end seal the roll completely.

III. Deep-frying

1. Heat oil to 375°. Fry folded spring rolls until golden brown.

2. Serve hot, plain or with vinegar, or with sweet and sour sauce. See below.

Sweet and Sour Sauce:

Bring to a boil a mixture of 4 T catsup, 4 T sugar, 4 T vinegar, 4 T water and 1 T cornstarch. Let cool before using.

Fried spring rolls can be kept in the refrigerator 2 or 3 days, or in the freezer for weeks when wrapped in a plastic bag. Before serving, reheat in a pre-heated oven at 300° for 5 to 8 minutes or until they are heated through.

20 spring rolls:

Calories: 2320   Carbohydrates: 219 gm
Protein: 78 gm   Fat: 124 gm

(Calculated with ground beef chuck and 4 T oil for deep-frying. Approximately 116 calories per spring roll.)

SWEET-RICE WINE DESSERT
(Tian Jiu Niang)

甜酒釀

Ingredients:

    2 lb glutinous rice
    ½ ball of sweet-wine yeast*

Method:

1. Roll the yeast into a fine powder.
2. Soak the rice in cold water for 4 hours. Drain in a strainer.
3. Place a layer of dampened cheese cloth in a tier of a steamer. Put the rice on the cheese cloth; steam over a boiling steamer for 1 hour.
4. Plunge the rice into cold, running water until the rice becomes thoroughly cold. Drain well.
5. Put the rice in a pan or a pot; add yeast powder and mix well. Press the rice gently until the surface becomes smooth.
6. Make a 3" hole in the middle of the rice from top to the bottom of the pan. Cover tightly and keep the container in a warm place. After 3-4 days the Sweet-Rice Wine Dessert is ready to serve (no peeking or disturbing it while it is fermenting). Serve cold plain or with fruit cocktail.

Sweet-rice wine dessert can be kept in the refrigerator for a long time. The equipment to be used for making this dessert should be **very** clean.

* The yeast is sold in some Oriental grocery stores in dried balls about ¾" in diameter and can be kept in a covered jar indefinitely. There is no other yeast substitute for this recipe. Use only the glutinous rice.

Two pounds of glutinous rice:

Calories: 3274   Carbohydrates: 724 gm
Protein: 50.8 gm   Fat: 8.2 gm

microwave oven

MICROWAVE CHINESE COOKING

In the past few years, microwave cooking has rapidly grown in popularity and usage. Although this method of cooking varies from conventional cooking, it is relatively easy to adjust to in a short time. Anyone who has had the experience of using a microwave oven will attest to its speed and clean cooking. Used properly, no spilling or spattering occurs.

Although several microwave oven cookbooks are available, there are *no* Chinese microwave oven cookbooks to my knowledge. A common notion is that Chinese cooking is too complicated and elaborate to be adapted to microwave cooking. Somehow, I was convinced that, if Chinese cooking can be adapted to cooking on electric or gas ranges, there should be a way to adapt it to microwave oven cooking.

After much thought, experimenting and tasting, I have succeeded in completing a section of authentic tasting Chinese recipes. I had to initiate new methods of the technique and concept of Chinese cooking in order to preserve the original flavors, but after much work, succeeded.

I am proud to present these recipes to you. They are delicious, nutritious, easy to follow, and attractive to the eye. These dishes will go well with rice or Chinese steamed bread.

Through my experiments, I found that the length of cooking time is not a great deal shorter than the stir-fry method, but the clean-up is definitely shorter and easier. Because constant stirring is not necessary while the food is in the microwave oven, the cook can be performing other tasks in preparation for the meal.

I have tested and retested these recipes to my complete satisfaction. Some of my friends also tried these recipes: Mrs. Mary Kooyers has faithfully tried all the recipes in her kitchen. She never failed to reach success with these recipes. Mrs. Anna Chapekis read my recipes and edited them for easier reading. To these friends, I sincerely express my appreciation and thanks.

How fortunate my family and I are to live in this fine university town, and to come in contact with so many educated and informed people.

I welcome comments or criticism from anyone who cares to share their thoughts with me. I take complete responsibility for any problems with these recipes, although I am sure you will not have any.

BEAN THREAD SOUP
(Fen Si Tang)

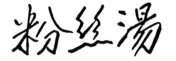

Ingredients:

½ lb pork loin or beef flank steak, sliced
1 T soy sauce
½ t onion powder
1 T sherry
1/8 t pepper
1 T cornstarch
1 carrot, peeled and sliced
1 C or more fresh spinach, cut into 2" pieces
2 t sesame oil
2 cans (13½-Fl oz) chicken or beef broth
2 oz bean thread, soaked
¼ minced ginger root

Method:

1. Soak bean thread in warm water for 20 minutes; drain cut into 2" sections.
2. Mix the first 5 ingredients together thoroughly; add cornstarch and mix well.
3. Place the last 3 ingredients in a deep, 3-quart container suitable for microwave cooking. Cook in microwave oven on full power for 12 minutes or until the soup boils.
4. Stir in meat and carrots; cover with plastic wrap and cook on full power for 2 minutes.
5. Add spinach and sesame oil (without cooking) and serve immediately.

Step 1 of the "method" can be prepared in advance.

(cont'd)

Calories: 495   Carbohydrates: 16gm
Protein: 29gm   Fat: 34gm

(Calculated with pork loin, also see page 20)

蝦仁湯   **SHRIMP SOUP**
             (Xia Ren Tang)

Ingredients:

 ¼ lb frozen raw shrimp, cleaned, deveined and thawed
 ¼ t salt
  1 t sherry
 ¼ t onion powder
1/8 t pepper
  2 t cornstarch
 ¼ lb pork loin, sliced
  1 T soy sauce
1/8 t pepper
1/8 t onion powder
  2 t cornstarch
  1 t sherry
 10 Wonton skins, cut into quarters
  2 oz frozen peas and carrots, thawed (about ½ C)
  2 t seasame oil

  Watercress for garnishing (optional)

  2 cans (13½ fl. oz) chicken or beef broth
8-10 water chestnuts, sliced
  2 thin slices of ginger root

(cont'd)

298

Method:

1. Mix the shrimp with the next 5 ingredients; set aside.
2. Mix the pork with the next 5 ingredients; set aside.
3. Place the last 4 ingredients in a deep, 3-quart container suitable for microwave cooking. Cook in microwave on full power for 12 minutes, or until it reaches a boil.
4. Add pork; Stir well. Cover with plastic wrap and cook full power for 2 minutes.
5. Add Wonton skins, one by one, quickly. Stir well. Cover and cook for 2 minutes on full power.
6. Add shrimp, peas and carrots; cover and cook on full power for 3 minutes.
7. Add sesame oil and garnish with watercress. Serve immediately. Steps 1 and 2 of the "method" can be prepared in advance.

Calories: 802   Carbohydrates: 58gm
Protein: 58gm   Fat: 35gm

牛肉菜花

BEEF WITH BROCCOLI
AND MUSHROOMS
(Niu Rou Cai Hua)

Ingredients:

¾ lb beef flank steak, sliced
3 T soy sauce
1/8 t pepper
½ t onion powder
1 T sherry
½ t brown sugar
½ t finely minced ginger root
2 T oil
1 T cornstarch
2 stalks of broccoli, cut into 1" pieces
¼ lb fresh mushrooms, sliced
2 green onions, shredded
1/3 t salt
1/8 t MSG (optional)
1 T oil

Method:

1. Mix the first 8 ingredients together thoroughly in a bowl; add cornstarch and mix well.

2. Toss gently the last 6 ingredients in a 2-quart casserole or container suitable for microwave cooking. Cover with plastic wrap and cook in microwave oven on full power for 2 minutes.

3. Spread the meat evenly over the vegetables; cover and cook on full power for 4 minutes. Mix well before serving.

4. Transfer the beef to a serving platter before serving if you wish.

Step 1 of the "method" can be prepared in advance.

Calories: 910   Carbohydrates: 23gm
Protein: 83gm   Fat: 62gm

BEEF WITH GREEN ONIONS
(Jing Cong Niu Rou)

京慈牛肉

Ingredients:

>   1   lb beef flank steak, sliced
>   3   T soy sauce
>   ¼   t pepper
>   1   T sherry
>   1   t brown sugar
>   ¼   t finely minced ginger root
>   3   T oil
>   1   T cornstarch
>   6-8 green onions, shredded
>   2   t sesame oil

Method:

1. Place the first 7 ingredients in a 2-quart container suitable for microwave cooking. Mix well.

2. Add cornstarch to the meat; mix well.

3. Cover the container with plastic wrap; cook in microwave oven on full power for 5 minutes. Stir thoroughly.

4. Spread the green onion shreds over the meat; cover the cook on full power for 3 minutes.

5. Add sesame oil and mix well. Serve hot.

Steps 1 and 2 of the "method" can be prepared in advance.

Calories: 1169   Carbohydrates: 14gm
Protein: 100gm   Fat: 76gm

海鮮肉片 **HOISIN SAUCE PORK WITH PEPPER**
(Hoisin Rou Pia)

Ingredients:

  1 lb pork loin, sliced
  1 T soy sauce
  ¼ C Hoisin sauce
  1 T sherry
1/8 t pepper
  ¼ t onion powder
  2 thin slices of ginger root
  3 T oil
  1 T cornstarch
  2 green onions, shredded
  1 large green pepper, cut into 1" squares
  ¼ t salt
  1 t sesame oil

Method:

1. Place the first 8 ingredients in a 2-quart container suitable for microwave cooking. Mix thoroughly.
2. Add cornstarch and mix well.
3. Cover the container with plastic wrap; cook in microwave oven on full power for 6 minutes. Stir well.
4. Spread green onions and green pepper evenly over the meat; sprinkle salt on green pepper; cover and cook on full power for 3 minutes.
5. Add sesame oil and mix well. Serve immediately.

Steps 1 and 2 of the "method" can be prepared in advance.

Calories: 1680   Carbohydrates: 12gm
Protein: 82gm   Fat: 142gm

PORK WITH VEGETABLES
(Chao Rou Pian)

Ingredients:

- ¾ lb pork loin, sliced
- 4 T soy sauce
- 1 T sherry
- 1/8 t pepper
- 3-4 cloves of garlic, crushed
- 1 t brown sugar
- 3 T oil
- 1 T cornstarch
- 1 t seasame oil
- 1 carrot, sliced
- 1 C sliced celery
- 2 green onions, shredded

Method:

1. Mix the first 7 ingredients together thoroughly in a 2-quart container suitable for microwave cooking.

2. Add cornstarch to the meat and mix well.

3. Cover the container with plastic wrap and cook in microwave oven on full power for 5 minutes.

4. Add the last 3 ingredients; cover and cook on full power for 3 minutes.

5. Add sesame oil and mix well; cover and cook the food for 1 minute. Serve hot.

Steps 1 and 2 the "method" can be prepared in advance.

Calories: 1400   Carbohydrates: 13gm
Protein: 64gm   Fat: 118gm

杏仁加厘雞

ALMOND CHICKEN
WITH CURRY
(Xing Ren Ka Li Ji)

Ingredients:

    1 lb boneless chicken breast, diced
    3 T soy sauce
    ½ t onion powder
  1/8 t pepper
    1 T sherry
    1 T curry powder, or more
    3 T oil
    1 T cornstarch
    ½ C toasted almonds, slivered, sliced or whole
    1 C frozen peas, thawed (about 5-6 oz)
    2 green onions, minced

Method:

1. Mix the first 7 ingredients thoroughly in a 2-quart container or casserole suitable for microwave cooking.

2. Add cornstarch to the chicken and mix well.

3. Cover the casserole with plastic wrap and cook in microwave oven on full power for 5 minutes. Mix.

4. Add the peas and green onions to the chicken; cover and cook in microwave oven on full power for 2 minutes.

5. Mix the chicken and vegetables well. Transfer the chicken to a serving platter and spread the almonds over the chicken. Serve hot.

Steps 1 and 2 of the "method" can be prepared in advance.

Calories: 1527   Carbohydrates: 57gm
Protein: 131gm   Fat: 91gm

BLACK BEAN CHICKEN WITH SNOW PEA PODS
(Dou Shi Xue Dou Ji)

Ingredients:

    1 lb boneless chicken breast, sliced
    3 T fermented black beans
    1 T soy sauce
    2 cloves of garlic, minced
    ¼ t finely minced ginger root
    ½ t brown sugar
    1 T sherry
    3 T oil
    1 T cornstarch
    1 carrot, sliced
    ¼ snow pea pods
      Salt and pepper to taste

Method:

1. Soak the fermented black beans in IT hot water for 5 minutes. Mash the soaked beans into paste.

2. Peel the carrot and slant slice. Set aside.

3. Wash and snap off the stems and strings from both ends of the snow pea pods. Set aside.

4. Place the first 8 ingredients in a 2-quart container, suitable for microwave cooking, mix thoroughly. Add cornstarch and mix well.

5. Cover the container with plastic wrap and cook in microwave oven on full power for 3 minutes.

6. Add carrots to the chicken and mix well. Cover and cook on full power for 1 minute. Mix well before serving.

Step 4 of the "method" can be prepared in advance.

Calories: 1178   Carbohydrate: 42gm
Protein: 122gm   Fat: 55gm

蠔油菜芽

**BRUSSELS SPROUTS
WITH OYSTER SAUCE**
(Hao You Cai Ya)

Ingredients:

    1 lb brussels sprouts
    1 t sesame oil
    2 slices of ginger root
    2 green onions, shredded
 1/8 t pepper
  ½ t brown sugar
    3 T oyster sauce
    3 T oil

Method:

1. Wash the brussels sprouts and trim off the stems and outer leaves. Cut the brussels sprouts into halves (cut into quarters if it is a large one).

2. Place the brussels sprouts in a 2-quart container suitable for microwave cooking.

3. Add the last 6 ingredients to the brussels sprouts. Toss gently so that the seasonings will penetrate the vegetables evenly.

4. Cover the container with plastic wrap; cook in microwave oven on full power for 3 minutes.

5. Stir the vegetables; cover and cook on full power for 3 minutes.

6. Stir the vegetables again; cover and cook on full power for another 3 minutes. Add sesame oil and serve hot.

Calories: 572   Carbohydrates: 34gm
Protein: 16gm   Fat: 43gm

RAINBOW SHRIMP
(Cai Hung Xia Ren)

彩虹蝦仁

Ingredients:

   ½ lb frozen raw shrimp, cleaned, deveined and thawed
   ¾ t salt
   ¼ t sugar
   ½ t onion powder
 1/8 t pepper
   1 T sherry
 1/8 t MSG (optional)
 1½ T oil
   1 T cornstarch
   2 t sesame oil
   2 green onions, minced
   1 carrot, peeled and slant sliced
 3-5 Chinese dried mushrooms, soaked and sliced
   1 large stalk of broccoli, washed and cut into 1" pieces
 6-7 water chestnuts, sliced
   2 slices of ginger root
 3/4 t salt
 1/8 t MSG (optional)
 1½ T oil
   1 T sherry

Method:

1. Mix the first 8 ingredients together thoroughly in a bowl; add cornstarch and mix well. Set aside.

2. Place the last 9 ingredients in a 2-quart container suitable for microwave cooking. Toss the ingredients gently; then cover with a sheet of plastic wrap and cook in microwave oven on full power for 2-3 minutes.

(cont'd)

3. Spread the shrimp evenly over the vegetables; cover and cook on full power for 4 minutes.

4. Add green onions and sesame oil; mix well. Serve hot.

Step 1 of the "method" can be prepared in advance.

Calories: 794   Carbohydrates: 24gm
Protein: 48gm   Fat: 54gm

PLAIN RICE
(Bai Fan)

Ingredients:

    1½ C rice, long or medium grain
    2½ C water

Method:

1. Place the rice in a 2-quart container cookware suitable for microwave cooking.

2. Add water, stir to make sure all the rice is moistened.

3. Cook the rice in microwave oven, uncovered, on full power for 10 minutes.

4. Cover the cookware with plastic wrap and cook on 50% power (simmer) for 10 minutes.

5. Let stand in the microwave oven for 2 minutes before serving. Serve hot.

Cold rice reheats very well in a microwave oven. To reheat, cover the rice with plastic wrap and heat on full power for 3-6 minutes.

Calories: 1005   Carbohydrates: 224gm
Protein: 18gm   Fat: 2gm

308

ALMOND PUDDING
(Xing Ren Bu Ding)

杏仁布丁

Ingredients:

 1 C almonds
 2½ C milk
 ½ - ¾ C sugar
 ½ t salt
 2 T cornstarch
 1 t almond extract
 ½ C whipping cream, whipped
 Candied cherries for garnishing (optional)

Method:

1. Toast the almonds in a 375⁰ pre-heated oven for 5-8 minutes. Let cool.

2. Place the first 5 ingredients in a blender; cover tightly and blend for 1 minute.

3. Pour the blended almond mixture into a deep, 3-quart container suitable for microwave cooking.

4. Cook the almond mixture in microwave oven, uncovered, for 5 minutes on full power.

5. Stir once and cook on full power for 3 minutes.

6. Cover the cookware with plastic wrap and cook on 30% power (defrost) for 4 minutes.

7. Stir in almond extract and let cool. Fold in whipped cream and garnish with candied cherry and serve cold.

Calories: 2053   Carbohydrates: 175gm
Protein: 52gm   Fat: 137gm

Chinese Ingredients and Seasonings

Abalone: A special kind of shellfish sold in cans in Oriental grocery stores. It is pre-cooked and ready to use.

Bamboo shoots: Ivory-colored tender shoots of bamboo, are sold in cans of different sizes in Oriental grocery stores or in supermarkets. After opening the can, transfer the bamboo shoots to a water-filled, covered jar and store in refrigerator for up to two weeks. Change the water once every two days.

Bean curd or To Fu: A highly nutritious vegetable protein made from soy beans. The creamy-colored, custard-like textured To Fu is sold in squares (approximately 1 pound per square) in Oriental grocery stores or in supermarkets. To Fu itself is tasteless but easily absorbs the flavor of other foods. It can be stored in the refrigerator in a water filled container for about ten days. Change the water daily.

Bean sprouts: The sprouts of mung beans or soy beans. Mung bean sprouts are more popular in America. They are sold in cans in supermarkets or fresh, by weight, in Oriental grocery stores. You can grow bean sprouts in your home (see page 185).

Bean threads: Also known as cellophane noodles or vermicelli noodles. They are made from ground mung beans. Bean threads are sold dry in small bundles of 1-6 oz packages in Oriental grocery stores or in some supermarkets. They can be kept for a long time in a dry place.

Bird's nest: Small pieces of translucent material of the nest of special sea swallows. They are sold in Oriental grocery stores by the ounce. They should be soaked and cleaned carefully according to package directions.

(cont'd)

Black beans: Fermented and highly seasoned black soy beans, sold in Oriental grocery stores in cans or in plastic bags. After opening, transfer to a tightly covered jar and store in the refrigerator for months.

Calcium sulfate: A white powdered chemical ($CaSO_4 \cdot 2H_2O$) sold in drug stores as well as hardware stores under the trade name "Plaster of Paris." Chinese use this powder to make bean curd (To Fu) from soy beans (see page 193).

Chestnuts: The sweet, edible nuts of the chestnut tree. The nut has a prickly bur shell, reddish brown in color. They are sold shelled and dried in Oriental grocery stores or fresh in supermarkets.

Cinnamon stick: Two inch long cinnamon sticks sold in supermarkets in the spice section are suitable for Chinese cooking.

Chinese cabbage: At least three varieties are available in the United States. One is called celery cabbage. It has tightly packed, yellowish stalks somewhat resembling celery and can be eaten raw as a salad or cooked. Another one is called Bok Choy. It has white, loosely packed stalks and large, dark green leaves. It cannot be eaten raw. A third one is called napa and can be eaten raw as well as cooked. It has loosely packed, yellowish wide leaves. All three varieties are sold fresh, by weight, in supermarkets and Oriental grocery stores.

Chinese or black or dried mushrooms: There are several kinds available and sold in Oriental grocery stores. One is dark in color and thin. The other one is light in color and thick, with cracks on the surface. Another type comes in broken pieces and is newly imported from mainland China. They are all good. Store in a dry place in a covered jar. Before using, soak the mushrooms in hot water for an hour or until they soften. Squeeze out water and remove the stems before using.

(cont'd)

Cooking fat: In China, lard is considered the best fat for cooking. It gives a rich flavor to the food. Peanut oil is considered the best vegetable oil for cooking because it is odorless. Since animal fats are high in cholesterol, I would not use lard to cook with. All vegetable oils (in the United States) are odorless; I suggest that you use any kind except olive and coconut oil.

Cooking wine: Pale dry sherry has the flavor closest to the rice cooking wine used in China. Chinese people use a very small amount of wine in cooking to improve the flavor as well as to cover up any unpleasant odor of the food.

Dried lily buds or golden needles: Flower buds of the lily, about 2-3 inches long. Sold in dried, pressed blocks or in plastic bags by weight. Store in covered container in a dry place for months.

Dried shrimp: Salted, shelled, dried shrimp have a strong sharp flavor. Produced in New Orleans or imported from the Orient, they are sold in Oriental grocery stores. They can be kept in a covered jar in a dry place for months.

Dried wood ear: A special kind of black or white fungus which grows on trees in China. It is sold dried in irregular sizes in Oriental grocery stores. Wood ear can be kept in a dry place for a long time.

Five-spice powder: A powdered mixture of five ground spices. They are fennel, star anise, clove, cinnamon and Szechwan peppercorn. It is sold by weight in Oriental grocery stores.

Garlic: The bulb of the garlic plant is used as seasoning, especially in the dishes of the Northern part of China.

Ginger root: Tube-like brown root with a spicy flavor. The Chinese believe that the strong aroma of the fresh ginger root can cover up and absorb unpleasant food odors. Discard the ginger root after cooking. Fresh
(cont'd)

312

ginger is sold in Oriental grocery stores and in some supermarkets. It can be kept several weeks in a plastic bag in the refrigerator. Peeled ginger root can be kept in dry sherry in the refrigerator for months.

Ginkgo nuts: The nuts of a large ornamental tree of China and Japan. They are sold in cans in Oriental stores and are ready to use.

Green onions or scallions: Sold in supermarkets, they are more popular than regular onions in Chinese cooking. Remove the roots and use the whole onion.

Hot pepper: Red chilies sold whole, as flakes or in a paste in Oriental grocery stores. The paste can be made at home (see page 184).

Hoisin sauce: A thick, brownish bean paste seasoned with spices and sold in cans. After opening, transfer the paste to a covered container and store in the refrigerator for months.

Lime: A strong alkaline material used to make thousand-years' eggs.

Litchi: A nut shaped fruit with a thin, hard, rough, red skin. Inside the shell is a sweet, white, edible jelly-like pulp with a single brown seed. It is sold in cans in Oriental grocery stores. Canned ones are ready to eat. The dried pulp should be soaked until they are soft before using.

Lotus root: The long ivory-colored root of the lotus plant. Sold fresh or in cans, in sections or in slices in Oriental grocery stores. The fresh ones should be kept in the refrigerator before using.

Monosodium Glutamate: A flavor enhancer sold in supermarkets under the trade name Accent or M.S.G. (see page 7).

Mushroom soy sauce: A newly imported soy sauce from the People's Republic of China and sold in Oriental

(cont'd)

grocery stores. The flavor is excellent. Use it the same way you would soy sauce.

Oyster sauce: A dark-colored, oyster-flavored, thick sauce that can be used the same way as soy sauce. Oyster sauce is saltier than soy sauce; reduce the quantity when using it.

Sea cucumber or bêche-de-mer: A cucumber-shaped, small creature of the sea, sold dried in Oriental grocery stores. Store it in a dry place indefinitely.

Sea weeds: The plants of the sea sold in Oriental grocery stores in dried form. There are different kinds of edible sea weeds; all are rich in iodine. They can be kept in a dry place indefinitely.

Sesame oil: A strong nutty-flavored oil from roasted sesame seeds, sold in bottles or cans in different sizes in Oriental grocery stores. It can be kept in a well sealed container for one year.

Shark's fin: Needle-like fragments from the fins of sharks sold dried, by weight, in Oriental grocery stores. Store in a dry place.

Snow peas or sugar peas: Pale green, flat, crisp young pea pods sold fresh in Oriental grocery stores and in some supermarkets. Snap off both ends and eat the peas, pods and all. Fresh pea pods can be wrapped and stored in the refrigerator for a few days. Frozen pea pods are also available in 10 oz boxes.

Sodium hydroxide (caustic soda): A strong alkaline chemical used to make thousand-years' eggs.

Soy sauce: Brownish, salty liquid made from fermented soy beans, wheat flour and salt. It is an important seasoning in Chinese cooking. It is sold in different sizes of bottles and cans in Oriental grocery stores and in supermarkets. *(cont'd)*

314

Star anise: A popular spice sold dry in Oriental grocery stores. The whole star anise contains 7-8 cloves and is shaped like a star. It can be kept in a dry place in a jar for years. There are no substitutes for star anise.

Szechwan peppercorn: A spice that looks like black peppercorn but is lighter in color and weight. It is sold whole in Oriental grocery stores. It can be kept in the cupboard indefinitely. There are no substitutes for Szechwan peppercorn.

Vinegar: A rich brownish rice vinegar from China which is sold in some Oriental grocery stores is the best. Apple cider vinegar can be substituted.

Water chestnuts: A vegetable that grows in a flooded field. The edible portion is the root bulb of the plant, about one inch in diameter with brownish skin and white meat. It is sold fresh by weight or in cans in Oriental grocery stores as well as in supermarkets. After opening canned water chestnuts, transfer to a water-filled covered jar and store in the refrigerator up to 3 weeks. Change the water once every two days. Never freeze water chestnuts.

Winter melon: Long melon with a pale-green skin. It is sold fresh in some Oriental grocery stores whole or by sections. The whole Winter melon looks like a long-shaped watermelon but has a tougher skin and a frosty, white powder on the surface. It can be kept in refrigerator for one week when wrapped in a plastic bag.

Tables and Charts

<table>
<tr><td>

ABBREVIATIONS

t: teaspoon(s)
T: tablespoon(s)
C: cup(s)
qt: Quart(s)
oz: ounce(s)
lb: pound(s)
min: minute(s)
hr: hour(s)
in: inch(es)
diam: diameter(s)
doz: dozen(s)
mg: milligram(s)
gm: gram(s)
kg: kilogram(s)

</td><td>

MEASUREMENTS

1 pinch: less than 1/8 teaspoon
1 tablespoon: 3 teaspoons
8 tablespoons: ½ cup
1 pint: 2 cups
1 quart: 2 pints
1 quart: 4 cups
1 gallon: 4 quarts: 128 ounces
1 fluid ounce: 2 tablespoons: 28.35 grams
1 pound: 16 ounces: 453.6 grams
100 grams: 3½ ounces
1 kilogram: 2.2 pounds
1 cup: 8 fluid ounces: ½ pint: 16 tablespoons
1 liter: 1.057 quarts

</td></tr>
</table>

SOURCES OF IMPORTANT NUTRIENTS

Important Nutrients	*Important Sources*
Protein	Meat, fish, eggs, poultry Milk and cheese Dried beans, peas and nuts Breads and cereals
Fat	Vegetable oils and dressings Meat fats and fat meats Butter and cream
Carbohydrates (Sugars and Starch)	Sugar, candy, jelly, jam, syrup, honey Breads, cereals, potatoes and corn Fresh and dried fruits

(cont'd)

Vitamins		
	Vitamin A	Liver, eggs, butter, cream Whole milk, fortified skim milk Dark green and deep yellow vegetables Deep yellow fruits
	The B Vitamins	Organ meats, meats, fish, poultry, eggs Milk, cheese, ice cream Whole grain and enriched breads and cereals Whole potatoes, dried beans Dark green leafy vegetables
	Vitamin C or Ascorbic Acid	Citrus fruits—lemon, lime, orange, grapefruit Fresh fruits and vegetables White potatoes
	Vitamin D or The Sunshine Vitamin	Vitamin D enriched milk, butter Fish liver oil Sunshine
Minerals		
	Calcium	Milk, cheese, ice cream Canned sardines, salmon (with bones) Broccoli, collard, kale Mustard and turnip greens
	Iodine	Sea weeds, seafoods Iodized salt

	Iron	Liver, egg yolk, meat
		Green leafy vegetables
		Prunes, raisins, strawberries,
		  blueberries
		Enriched or whole grain bread
		  and cereals
		Dried apricots

WEIGHT IN POUNDS ACCORDING TO FRAME
IN INDOOR CLOTHING

Selected desirable weights for men of ages 25 and over

Height (with 1-inch shoes on)	Small frame	Medium frame	Large frame
5 ft. 5 in.	121-129	127-139	135-152
5 ft. 6 in.	124-133	130-143	138-156
5 ft. 7 in.	128-137	134-147	142-161
5 ft. 8 in.	132-141	138-152	147-166
5 ft. 9 in.	136-145	142-156	151-170
5 ft. 10 in.	140-150	146-160	155-174
5 ft. 11 in.	144-154	150-165	159-179
6 ft.	148-158	154-170	164-184
6 ft. 1 in.	152-162	158-175	168-189
6 ft. 2 in.	156-167	162-180	173-194

Selected desirable weights for women of ages 25 and over

Height (with 2-inch shoes on)	Small frame	Medium frame	Large frame
5 ft.	96-104	101-113	109-125
5 ft 1 in.	99-107	104-116	112-128
5 ft. 2 in.	102-110	107-119	115-131
5 ft. 3 in.	105-113	110-122	118-134
5 ft. 4 in.	108-116	113-126	121-138
5 ft. 5 in.	111-119	116-130	125-142
5 ft. 6 in.	114-123	120-135	129-146
5 ft. 7 in.	118-127	134-139	133-150
5 ft. 8 in.	122-131	128-143	137-154
5 ft. 9 in.	126-135	132-147	141-158

(From Metropolitan Life Insurance Co.)

To lose one pound of body fat requires a reduction of about 3,500 calories.

DAILY DIETARY REQUIREMENTS OF CALORIES, CERTAIN VITAMINS AND MINERALS [*]

Calories: 2333
Protein: 51 gm
Calcium: 800 mg
Iron: 12.6 mg
Vitamin A: 4,500 I.U.
Thiamine (vit. B$_1$): 1.2 mg
Riboflavin (vit. B$_2$): 1.4mg
Niacin: 15 mg
Ascorbic acid (*vit. C*): 45 mg

[*] Condensed from Recommended Daily Dietary Allowances, Food and Nutrition Board, National Research Council, Revised 1974.
For men and women, ages 19-51+, averaged.
Designed for maintenance of good nutrition of practically all healthy persons in the U.S.A. Allowances are intended for persons normally active in a temperate climate.

TABLES OF FOOD COMPOSITION BASED ON 100 Gm OF EDIBLE PORTION
(Calories, protein, fat and carbohydrates only)

Name	Approximate composition			
	Cal-ories	Pro-tein Gm.	Fat Gm.	Carbo-hydrates Gm.
Abalone, canned	80	16.0	.3	2.3
Almonds, dried	598	18.6	54.2	19.5
Asparagus, raw spears	26	2.5	.2	5.0
Bacon, cured raw	665	8.4	69.3	1.0
Bamboo shoots, raw	27	2.6	.3	5.2

TABLES OF FOOD COMPOSITION BASED ON
100 Gm OF EDIBLE PORTION
(Calories, protein, fat and carbohydrates only)

Name	Approximate composition			
	Cal-ories	Pro-tein Gm.	Fat Gm.	Carbo-hydrates Gm.
Banana, raw, common	85	1.1	.2	22.2
Bass, white, raw	98	18.0	2.3	0
Beans, dry, red, raw	343	22.5	1.5	61.9
Beans, mung, dry, raw	340	24.2	1.3	60.3
Beans, mung, sprouted, uncooked	35	3.8	.2	6.6
Beef:				
chuck, 82% lean, 18% fat, raw	257	18.7	19.6	0
flank steak, raw	139	21.8	5.1	0
ground, regular	268	17.9	21.2	0
Bird's nest		54.3	.3	23.3
Bouillon cubes	120	20	3.	5.
Breads, enriched, white	269	8.7	3.2	50.4
Broccoli, spears, raw	32	3.6	.3	5.9
Brussels sprouts, raw	45	4.9	.4	8.3
Cabbage, common varieties, raw	24	1.3	.2	5.4
Cabbage, Chinese	14	1.2	.1	3.0
Carrots, raw	42	1.1	.2	9.7
Cauliflower, raw	27	2.7	.2	5.2
Celery, raw	17	.9	.1	3.9
Chicken, fryer, ready to cook (refuse: bones)	84.2	12.6	3.3	0
breast, raw (refuse: bones)	86.8	16.4	1.8	0
drumstick, raw (refuse: bones)	69	11.2	2.3	0
thigh, raw (refuse: bones)	93.6	13.6	4.2	0
wing, raw (refuse: bones)	71.6	9.1	3.6	0
Corn, sweet, frozen	82	3.1	.5	19.7
Cornstarch	362	.3	Trace	87.6
Cucumber, pared, raw	14	.6	.1	3.2
Duck, total edible	326	16.0	28.6	0

TABLES OF FOOD COMPOSITION BASED ON
100 Gm OF EDIBLE PORTION
(Calories, protein, fat and carbohydrates only)

Name	Approximate composition			
	Cal-ories	Pro-tein Gm.	Fat Gm.	Carbo-hydrates Gm.
Egg:				
chicken, whole	163	12.9	11.5	.9
duck, whole	191	13.3	14.5	.7
Fruit cocktail, canned,				
heavy syrup	76	.4	.1	19.7
Garlic, cloves, raw	137	6.2	.2	30.8
Gelatin, dry	335	85.6	.1	0
Ginger root, fresh	49	1.4	1.0	9.5
Heart:				
beef, raw	108	17.1	3.6	.7
hog	113	16.8	4.4	.4
Honey, strained	304	.3	0	82.3
Lard	902	0	100	0
Leek, raw	52	2.2	.3	11.2
Lettuce, crisp head	13	.9	.1	2.9
Lily buds				
Liver, raw				
beef	140	19.9	3.8	5.3
chicken	129	19.7	3.7	2.9
hog	131	20.6	3.7	2.6
Lotus root	49	1.7	.1	11.3
Lotus seeds	351	17.2	2.4	66.6
Litchis, raw	64	.9	.3	16.4
Milk, cow, whole	65	3.5	3.5	4.9
Mung bean thread				
Mushroom, raw	28	2.7	.3	4.4
Mustard greens, raw	31	3.0	.5	5.6
frozen	20	2.3	.4	3.2
Ocean perch, red fish	88	18.0	1.2	0

TABLES OF FOOD COMPOSITION BASED ON 100 Gm OF EDIBLE PORTION

(Calories, protein, fat and carbohydrates only)

Name	Approximate composition			
	Cal-ories	Pro-tein Gm.	Fat Gm.	Carbo-hydrates Gm.
Oil, salad or cooking	884	0	100.	0
Onion, mature, raw	38	1.5	.1	8.7
Onion, young, green	36	1.5	.2	8.2
Orange, raw, peeled	49	1.0	.2	12.2
Parsley, raw	44	3.6	.6	8.5
Peas, edible-pod, raw	53	3.4	.2	12.0
Peas, green, frozen	73	5.4	.3	12.8
Peas and carrots, frozen	55	3.3	.3	10.4
Pepper, hot chili,				
immature, raw pods	37	1.3	.2	9.1
mature, dried pods	321	12.9	9.1	59.8
Pepper, sweet, raw	22	1.2	.2	4.8
Pike, walleye, raw	93	19.3	1.2	0
Pineapple, canned, heavy syrup	74	.3	.1	19.4
Pork, Boston butt, 83% lean;				
17% fat, raw	251	16.5	20.0	0
Pork, spareribs, thin,				
total edible, raw	331	15.3	29.5.	0
Pork, dry ham, lean	310	19.5	25.0	.3
Pork, light cured ham, medium fat	282	17.5	23.0	0
Potatoes, raw	76	2.1	.1	17.1
Pumpkin seeds, dry	553	29.0	46.7	15.0
Radishes, Oriental	19	.9	.1	4.2
Rice, white enriched	363	6.7	.4	80.4
glutinous, raw	361	5.6	.9	79.8
Sausage, pork, dried, Oriental	603	17.0	58.3	3.6
Sea cucumber				
Sea weeds, raw, all varieties	-	-		-

TABLES OF FOOD COMPOSITION BASED ON
100 Gm OF EDIBLE PORTION
(Calories, protein, fat and carbohydrates only)

Name	Approximate composition			
	Cal-ories	Pro-tein Gm.	Fat Gm.	Carbo-hydrates Gm.
Sesame seeds, dry	563	18.6	49.1	21.6
Shark's fin, dried	384	89.4	.2	.1
Shrimp, fresh, shelled	84	17.9	.8	.1
dried	295	62.4	2.3	1.8
Soybeans, dry	403	34.1	17.7	33.5
Fermented product	167	16.9	7.4	11.5
Soybean curd (To Fu)	72	7.8	4.2	2.4
Soy bean sprouts, raw	46	6.2	1.4	5.3
Soy sauce	68	5.6	1.3	9.5
Sugars:				
brown	373	0	0	96.4
granulated	385	0	0	99.5
powdered	385	0	0	99.5
Sunflower seeds, dry	560	24.0	47.3	19.9
Tomatoes, ripe, raw	22	1.1	.2	4.7
Tomato catsup	106	2.0	.4	25.4
Tomato paste	82	3.4	.4	18.6
Tongue, raw, medium fat				
beef	207	16.4	15.0	.4
hog	215	16.8	15.6	.5
Turnips, raw	30	1.0	.2	6.6
Vinegar, cider	14	Trace	0	5.9
Walnuts:				
black	628	20.5	59.3	14.8
Persian or English	651	14.8	64.0	15.8
Water chestnut, raw	79	1.4	.2	19.0
Wheat flour, white	364	10.5	1.0	76.1
Winter melon				
Wood ears, dry				

Recipe Index

SOUP
Bean thread and dried shrimp soup 30
Bean thread and meat ball soup 31
Bird's nest soup 37
Cucumber soup 26
Egg drop soup 24
Noodle soup with assorted vegetables 32
Pickled Mustard green soup 27
Sesame flavored chicken soup 28
Shark's fin soup 36
Sparerib soup with soybean sprouts 40
Velvet corn soup 25
Winter melon soup 29
Wonton Soup 34

MEAT
Ant nest 61
Asparagus with beef 42
Barbecued spareribs 81
Beef and onion 60
Beef and string beans 43
Beef and bean sprouts 47
Beef with Bok Choy 44
Beef with curry 50
Beef with green pepper 46
Beef with mushrooms 49
Braised beef 53
Braised beef tongue 54
Braised pork hock or pork shoulder 82
Chow-Chow beef 51
Double cooked pork 92
Dried beef slices 57
Fluffy dried pork 78
Hoisin sauce pork 90
Lion's head (Large meat balls) 93
Liver with snow pea pods 72
Meat and soybean sprouts 73

Meat stuffed wheat gluten 66
Meat with pickled mustard greens 76
Moo Shu pork or beef 74
Pearl meat balls 69
Pork and shrimp chop suey 89
Pork with crushed garlic 77
Red broiled pork 86
Sautéed beef heart 56
Shredded beef chop suey 58
Snow peas with beef slices 48
Steamed black bean spareribs 79
Steamed ground meat 67
Steamed meat in noodle case 64
Stir-fry pork loin with green onion 85
Stuffed cucumber 63
Sweet and sour meat balls 70
Sweet and sour pork 87
Sweet and sour spareribs 80
White cut meat 84

POULTRY
Barbecued chicken wings 118
Bean sprouts and chicken salad 119
Black bean chicken 97
Chicken and nuts 111
Chicken breast with black walnuts 113
Chicken breast with Hoisin sauce 114
Chicken Foo Young 108
Chicken with almonds 116
Chicken with chestnuts 103
Chicken with curry 98
Fried spiced chicken 96
Lotus leaf rolls 129
Mo Go Gai Pien 110
Mushroom chicken 105
Oil dripping chicken 100
Peking duck 125
Salted cold chicken 102
Sautéed chicken wings 117
Smoked chicken 107
Soy sauce chicken 115

Stewed duck.................................120
Sweet rice stuffed duck (or Eight Precious duck) 123
Szechwan duck 121
Ta-Chan chicken.................................106
White cut chicken 99
Wined chicken.................................104

SEAFOOD
Abalone with snow pea pods and mushrooms.....................158
Braised shrimp in tomato sauce 145
Fish balls in brown sauce 142
Fish fillet with tomato sauce.........................139
Fish with meat shreds 132
Fluffy dried fish.........................144
Foil wrapped fish 138
Fried smelt fish 137
Happy family and reunion 159
Lobster Cantonese style 154
Phoenix tailed shrimps 148
Sautéed lobster tail 157
Shrimp balls.........................151
Shrimp omelet 153
Shrimp toast.........................150
Shrimp with cashews 146
Shrimp with green peas and tomato 147
Smoked fish 136
Soy sauce fish 135
Steamed fish.........................134
Steamed fish with black beans 141
Sweet and sour lobster 155

VEGETABLES
Asparagus salad 179
Baby cucumber Szechwan style 173
Braised mushrooms 175
Braised wheat gluten.........................188
Broccoli Chinese style 167
Brussels sprouts with meat sauce 168
Cabbage Chinese style 169
Cabbage with cream sauce.........................170

Cauliflower with soy sauce 172
Celery and dried shrimp salad 180
Country salad 181
Dried shrimp and turnip 178
Dry cooked string beans 165
Home grown bean sprouts 185
Hot pepper paste 184
Pickled mustard greens 183
Pickled spicy vegetables 182
Sautéed fresh mushrooms 174
Sautéed snow pea pods 176
Sautéed spinach 177
Stir-fry Bok Choy 166
String beans Chinese style 164
Sweet and sour cabbage 171
Vegetarian's delight 189
Wheat gluten (vegetable steaks) 186

BEAN CURD
Bamboo shoots with bean curd 210
Bean curd 193
Bean curd Foo Young 199
Bean curd soup 213
Bean curd with assorted meat and vegetables 196
Bean curd with fish in earthenware pot 215
Bean curd with pickled greens 209
Bean curd with smoked fish 217
Bean curd wtih vegetables 202
Black bean To Fu 203
Cold bean curd 207
Dry bean curd 195
Fried bean curd, plain 194
Hot bean curd 204
Hot and sour To Fu soup 211
Ma Po To Fu (bean curd) 205
Meat stuffed fried bean curd 200
Meat with dry bean curd 198
Shrimp bean curd 214
Soy sauce fried bean curd 206
Spiced dry bean curd 196
Spinach with bean curd 208

RICE, NOODLES AND CHINESE STEAMED BREAD

Boiled rice 220
Chicken rice 222
Chinese steamed bread 238
Cold noodles 234
Curried beef rice 227
Egg Noodles 233
Eighth of the twelve month rice chowder. 230
Fried noodles, (Chow Mein), crisp type 237
Fried noodles, (Chow Mein), soft type 235
Fried rice with assorted vegetables and ham 228
Home made noodles 231
Red broiled pork rice 226
Rice with crab or lobster meat 223
Sausage rice. 225
Shrimp rice 224
Steamed rice 221

EGGS

Egg dumplings 244
Egg omelet and beef rolls. 246
Egg omelet with pork and dried shrimp 247
Egg shreds. 242
Ham egg Foo Young 249
Onion scrambled eggs. 244
Pickled eggs. 252
San Hung Dan 255
Steamed meat with pickled eggs. 253
Tea eggs. 250
Thousand years' eggs. 254
Thousand years' eggs with soy sauce 256
Tomato scrambled eggs 243

DESSERTS AND SNACKS (Dim-Sum)

Almond bean curd. 262
Almond cookies 270
Banana in mink coat 264
Bean paste pan cake 272
Black beauty 266
Chinese pan cake 127
Chinese tea 259

Eight treasures rice pudding 267
Fried Wonton.. 287
Green onion crisp pancake...................................... 284
Home made donuts 273
Meat dumplings: 278
       boiled... 282
       fried.. 283
       steamed 283
Meat stuffed steamed buns..................................... 275
Meat stuffed pan-fried buns 276
Red bean paste.. 269
Red broiled pork stuffed buns 277
Sesame seed candy.. 260
Spring rolls (egg rolls)... 290
Spring roll and Wonton skins 286
Steamed cake 271
Sweet buns 274
Sweet-rice wine dessert.. 258
Walnut candies 261
Walnut soup dessert 263
White (silver) wood ear soup dessert 265

MICROWAVE CHINESE COOKING
Beef with broccoli and mushrooms 297
Beef with green onions 298
Hoisin sauce port with green pepper 299
Pork with vegetables.. 300
Black bean chicken with snow pea pods 301
Almond chicken with curry..................................... 302
Rainbow shrimp... 303
Brussels sprouts with oyster sauce.............................. 304
Bean thread soup 305
Shrimp soup 306
Plain rice.. 307
Almond pudding 308

RECIPES WHICH COULD BE SERVED AS APPETIZERS AND HORS D'OEUVRES

Barbecued chicken wings 118
Barbecued spareribs 81
Braised beef 53
Braised beef tongue 54
Braised mushrooms 175
Braised wheat gluten 188
Chow-Chow beef 51
Dried beef slices 57
Fried Wonton 287
Pearl meat balls 69
Red Broiled pork 86
Salted cold chicken 102
Sauteed chicken wings 117
Shrimp balls 151
Shrimp toast . . . . .15)
Smoked fish 136
Soy sauce fried bean curd 206
Spiced dry bean curd 196
Spring rolls (egg rolls) 290
Steamed meat in noodles case 64
Sweet and sour meat balls 70
Tea eggs 250
Thousand years' eggs with soy sauce 256
White cut chicken 99
Wined chicken 104

DINNER SUGGESTIONS

The following 6 menus are chosen as samples for a dinner of 4-5 men of ages 23-50.

(1) Cucumber soup (p. 26)
Beef with mushrooms (p. 49)
Broccoli Chinese style (p. 167)
Rice (p. 220)
Almond bean curd (dessert) (p. 262)

(2) Velvet corn soup (p. 25)
Chicken and nuts (p. 111)
Brussels sprouts with meat sauce (p. 168)
Rice (p. 220)
Almond bean curd (dessert) (p. 262)

(3) Egg drop soup (p. 24)
Fish fillet with tomato sauce (p. 139)
Stir-fry Bok Choy (p. 166)
Rice (p. 220)
Sesame seed candy (dessert) (p. 260)

(4) Bean curd soup (p. 213)
Shrimp and green peas and tomato (p. 147)
Fried rice with assorted vegetables and ham (p. 228)
Asparagus salad (p. 179)
Almond cookies (dessert) (p. 270)

(5) Velvet corn soup (p. 25)
Sweet and sour pork (p. 87)
Broccoli Chinese style (p. 167)
Rice (p. 220)
Sesame seed candy (dessert) (p. 260)

(6) Bean curd soup (p. 213)
Stir-fry pork with green onions (p. 85)
Broccoli Chinese style (p. 167)
Almond cookies (dessert) (p. 260)

The 6 menus given above have been evaluated in terms of amounts of specific nutrients. They would meet the daily requirement of calories but not exceed the body's need. The protein as the most important nutrient is adequately supplied both from vegetables and meats. The vitamins, minerals and fibers are sufficiently provided. The cholesterol level is low because a small amount of meat and vegetable oil is used in the cooking. The meal itself is not only delicious, but healthy, nutritious and well balanced.

MENUS EVALUATED IN TERMS OF SPECIFIC NUTRIENTS

MENU (1)

Calories and nutrients per menu		% of RDA* for man, age 23-50	
		1/4 of the menu **	1/5 of the menu **
1. Calories	3767	34%	28%
2. Nutrients:			
Carbohydrate	402 g	-	-
Protein	189 g	83%	68%
Fat	155 g	-	-
Cholesterol	442 mg	-	-
Calcium	1366 mg	42%	34%
Iron	37.5 mg	90%	75%
Vit. B1	3.3 mg	57%	46%
Vit. B2	5.1 mg	79%	63%
Vit. A	16100 IU	80%	64%
Vit. C	670 mg	370%	290%
Fiber	13.7 g	-	-

MENU (2)

Calories and nutrients per menu		% of RDA * for man, age 23-50	
		1/4 of the menu**	1/5 of the menu**
1. Calories	4170	38%	30%
2. Nutrients:			
Carbohydrate	495 g	-	-
Protein	213 g	94%	75%
Fat	158 g	-	-
Cholesterol	439 mg	-	-
Calcium	1241 mg	38%	31%
Iron	29.6 mg	70%	60%
Vit. B1	2.5 mg	42%	36%
Vit. B2	4.2 mg	65%	53%
Vit. A	6408 IU	32%	24%
Vit. C	617 mg	342%	270%
Fiber	13.5 g	-	-

* Recommended Dietary Allowances, 1974 8th Ed.
National Academy of Sciences, Washington D.C.

** Each man receives 1/4 or 1/5 of the total as shown in %
respectively, since the menu is designed for 4 or 5 men.

MENU (3)

Calories and nutrients per menu	% of RDA * for man, age 23-50	
	1/4 of the menu**	1/5 of the menu**
1. Calories 3808	35%	28%
2. Nutrients:		
Carbohydrate 397 g	-	-
Protein 148 g	66%	52%
Fat 182 g	-	-
Cholesterol 844 mg	-	-
Calcium 1295 mg	40%	32%
Iron 25.4 mg	60%	50%
Vit. B1 2.98 mg	50%	36%
Vit. B2 2.4 mg	37%	31%
Vit. A 3328 IU	16%	13%
Vit. C 104 mg	57%	46%
Fiber 11 g	-	-

MENU (4)

Calories and nutrients per menu	% of RDA* for man, age 23-50	
	1/4 of the menu**	1/5 of the menu**
1. Calories 3952	36%	29%
2. Nutrients:		
Carbohydrate 304 g	-	-
Protein 199 g	87%	69%
Fat 214 g	-	-
Cholesterol 1211 mg	-	-
Calcium 1041 mg	32%	26%
Iron 38 mg	95%	76%
Vit. B1 4.3 mg	71%	57%
Vit. B2 2.7 mg	43%	31%
Vit. A 21513 IU	107%	86%
Vit. C 247 mg	135%	108%
Fiber 12 g	-	-

  * Recommended Dietary Allowances, 1974 8th Ed.
National Academy of Sciences, Washington D.C.
** Each man receives 1/4 or 1/5 of the total as shown in %
respectively, since the menu is designed for 4 or 5 men.

MENU (5)			
Calories and nutrients per menu		% of RDA* for man, age 23-50	
		1/4 of the menu**	1/5of the menu**
1. Calories 4533		41%	35%
2. Nutrients:			
Carbohydrate	569 g	-	-
Protein	163 g	71%	57%
Fat	186 g	-	-
Cholesterol	570 mg	-	-
Calcium	1564 mg	48%	39%
Iron	37 mg	90%	70%
Vit. B1	6.3 mg	107%	85%
Vit. B2	4.2 mg	62%	50%
Vit A	17347 IU	86%	69%
Vit. C	739 mg	406%	326%
Fiber	14.7 g	-	-

MENU (6)			
Calories and nutrients per menu		% of RDA* for man, age 23-50	
		1/4 of the menu**	1/5 of the menu**
1. Calories 4030		37%	29%
2. Nutrients:			
Carbohydrate	274 g	-	-
Protein	165 g	73%	59%
Fat	251 g	-	-
Cholesterol	452 mg	-	-
Calcium	1116 mg	34%	27%
Iron	37 mg	90%	70%
Vit. B1	6.5 mg	114%	92%
Vit. B2	3.4 mg	53%	43%
Vit. A	15399 IU	76%	61%
Vit. C	653 mg	360%	280%
Fiber	10.9 g	-	-

* Recommended Dietary Allowances, 1974 8th Ed. National Academy of Sciences, Washington D.C.

** Each man receives 1/4 or 1/5 of the total as shown in % respectively, since the menu is designed for 4 or 5 men.

References

MSG, NUTRITION, AND SOYBEANS

Bean, L.H.: Closing the World's Nutritional Gap with Animal or Vegetable Protein. FAO Bull. 6. 1966

Bogert, L.J., et al: Nutrition and Physical Fitness, 8th edition. Saunders Company. 1966

Fd. Cosmet. Toxical. Vol. 11, pp. 309-321; More Meditation on MSG. Pergamon Press. 1973

FDA Report on Monosodium Glutamate, Nov. 17, 1969

Furia, T.E., ed: Handbook of Food Additives. Chemical Rubber Company, Clveland. 1968

Jacobson, M.F.: Eater's Digest. The Consumer's Factbook of Food Additives. Anchor Books. 1972

Lappe, F.M.: A Diet for a Small Planet. Ballantine Books, Inc. N.Y. 1971

Mitchell, H.S., et al: Nutrition in Health and Disease, 16th edition. Lippincott Company. 1976

NAS-NRC Food Protection Committee Report: Safty and Suitability of MSG for Use in Baby Foods. July, 1970

National Academy of Science: Recommended Daily Dietary Allowances. 8th edition. 1974

National Dairy Council: A Source Book on Food Practices. 1971

Nut. Rev. 28 124 158 (1970)

Piltz, Alber Ph.D.: How Your Body Uses Food, National Dairy Council, 1971

Report of a Joint FAO/WHO: Protein Requirements. Rome. 1965

Schaumburg, H.H., M.D.: New England J. of Med., 279 105, 1967

Science 170 549 (1970)

Science 163 825 (1969)

Smith and Circle: Soybeans: Chemistry and Technology. Volume 1, Proteins. The Avi Publishing Company, Inc. 1972

Stare, Fredrick: Eating for Good Health, Cornerstore Library, New York, 1969

United States Department of Agriculture, Bureau of Human Nutrition and Home Economics: Composition of Foods Used in Far Eastern Countries. Agriculture Handbook No. 34

United States Department of Agriculture, Home and Garden Bulletin: Nutritive Value of Foods. No. 72

United States Department of Agriculture, Agriculture Handbook: Composition of Foods, Raw, Processed, Prepared. No. 8

Wogan, G.N. Prof. MIT: Report on Monosodium Glutamate. Sept. 6, 1971

Wolfe, W.J., et al: Soybeans As a Food Source. CRC Press, 1970

The Year Book of Agriculture: Protecting Our Food. 1973

General Index

Abalone, 158, 310
Additives, 7
Almonds, 111, 116, 262, 270
Amino acids, 4-5
Anise, star, 53, 54, 57, 82, 312, 315
Appetizers, 12, 257-294, 330
Asparagus, 42, 179

Bamboo shoots, 310
Bananas, 264
Barbecued, 81, 118
Bass, 132, 134, 135, 141
Bean curd (To Fu) 193-217, 310
Bean paste, 267, 269, 272, 274
Bean sprouts, 40, 47, 73, 119, 185, 310
Bean threads, 30, 31, 61, 215, 310
Bird's nest, 37, 310
Biscuits, 273
Black beans, 79, 97, 141, 154, 184, 203, 311
Bok Choy, 44, 166, 202, 311
Braising, 14, 53, 54, 82, 145, 175
Bread, 169, 170, 171, 238
Broccoli, 167
Brussels sprouts, 168
Buns, 19, 169, 170, 171

Cabbage, 169, 170, 311
Cakes, 127, 271, 272, 284
Calcium, 18, 19
Calcium Sulfate, 193, 311
Calories, 2, 6, 18, 19, 20, 319-323
Candies, 260, 261
Carbohydrates, 2, 18, 316, 319-323
Cauliflowers, 172
Celery, 180
Cheese, 5
Chicken, 96-120, soup, 28
Chinese Restaurant Syndrome, 7-8
Chestnuts, 103, 311
Cholesterol, 5-6
Chopsticks, 10

Chop Suey, 58, 89
Chow Mein, 235, 237
Cinnamon, 107, 311, 312
Cleavers, 15
Cloud ear, see wood ear
Confucius, 1
Cookies, 270
Corn, 25
Crabmeat, 223
Cucumbers, 26, 63, 173, 182
Curry, 20, 50, 98, 227
Customs, 10-12
Cutting, 13

Desserts, 258, 260, 262-267, 270, 271, 273
Dim Sum, 257-294
Dried Cabbage, 83
Duck, 120-129
Dumplings, 244, 278-283

Eggs, 242-256
Fats, 2, 5, 6, 312, 316, 319-323
Fatty acids, 5
Five-spice powder, 144, 196, 312
Fried rice, 222-228
Frying, deep, pan, stir, 14

Garlic, 77, 312
Ginkgo nuts, 230, 313
Ginger roots, 313
Glutinous (sweet or sticky) rice, 69, 123, 258, 267

Hoisin sauce, 20, 313
Honey, 125
Hot pepper (chili), 58, 92, 106, 173, 184, 204, 313
Hua Chao, see Szechwan peppercorn

Infant, 8-9
Ingredients, 310-315

Lard, 312
Lily buds (golden needles), 20, 32
 74, 189, 211, 265, 312
Lion's head, 93
Litchi, 262, 313
Lobsters, 154-157
Lotus, leaf rolls, 129
 roots, 189, 313
 seeds, 123, 267

Meats, 42-94
Menus, planning, 17
 samples, 21-22
Method of preparation and
 cooking, 13-14
Microwave, 295-309
Minerals, 2, 18, 317, 319
Monosodium glutamate (Accent),
 2, 7-9, 313
Mung beans, 74, 185, 234, 235,
 237, 310
Mushrooms, 49, 105, 174, 175, 311
Mushroom soy sauce, 313
Mustard greens, 27, 76, 183, 198

Noodles, 18, 231-238
Nutrition, 2, 4, 18, 19

Omelets, 153, 246, 247
Oil, 295
Oysters, 153,
 sauce, 297

Pancakes, 127, 284
Pepper, green, 16
Pickled, egg, 67, 252, 255
 greens, 27, 76, 183, 209
 Vegetables, 182
Plum sauce, 149
Protein, 2, 4-5, 316, 319-323
Pudding, 267
Pumpkin seeds, 12

Quo Tie, 283

Radish, 181
Recipe index, 324-329

Rice, 10, 220-229
 wine dessert, 258
 Glutinous, 69, 123, 258, 267
Rolls, spring (egg), 290
 lotus leaf, 129

Salad, 119, 179, 180, 181
Sauces, Hoisin, 313
 Mustard, 287
 sweet and sour, 287
Sea cucumber, 20, 157, 314
Sesame seeds, 260, 264, 266, 314
 oil, 314
Sea weeds, 189, 314
Sherry, 312
Shark's fin, 1, 314
 soup, 36
Shrimps, 145-153, dried, 312
Smelt, 137
Smoked, 107, 136
Snacks, 258-294
Snow pea pods, 48, 72, 176, 314
Soups, 24-40, 211
Soybean sprouts, 40, 73, 185, 310
Soy sauce, 314
Spaghetti, 234, 235
Spareribs, 40, 79-81
Spring (egg) roll skin, 286
Steamer, 16
Steaming, 14
String beans, 43, 181, 182
Sweet and sour, 70, 81, 87, 139,
 155, 171
Szechwan, duck, 121
 pepper corns, 107, 121, 173, 182,
 215, 315

Tea, 10-12, 259
Tea egg, 250
Thousand-years' eggs, 254, 256
Tongue, 54
Turkey, 125
Turnips, 178

Utensils, 15

Vegetables, 164-190
Vinegar, 315
Vitamins, 2, 18, 317, 319

Walnuts, 111, 113, 261, 263
Water chestnuts, 315
Watermelon seeds, 12, 267
Wheat gluten, 66, 186, 188, 189
Wine, dessert, 258
    chicken, 104
Winter melon, 20, 315, soup, 29
Wonton, 34, 287
Wonton folding, 289
Wonton skin, 286
    revival, 287
Wok, 15
Wood ears, (cloud ears), 20, 32,
    74, 189, 211, 265, 312

Yeast, 238

- -

ORDER FORM

Christine Liu
P.O. Box 1332
Ann Arbor, Michigan 48106

Please send _____ copies of **Nutrition and Diet with Chinese Cooking** at $12.95 per copy (plus $2.00 for postage and handling). Payment should be enclosed with order.

Name _____

Address _____

City _____ State _____ Zip _____

Enclosed is _____ check or money order. Autographed copy ☐

- -

ORDER FORM

Christine Liu
P.O. Box 1332
Ann Arbor, Michigan 48106

Please send _____ copies of **Nutrition and Diet with Chinese Cooking** at $12.95 per copy (plus $2.00 for postage and handling). Payment should be enclosed with order.

Name _____

Address _____

City _____ State _____ Zip _____

Enclosed is _____ check or money order. Autographed copy ☐

- -

ORDER FORM

Christine Liu
P.O. Box 1332
Ann Arbor, Michigan 48106

Please send _____ copies of **Nutrition and Diet with Chinese Cooking** at $12.95 per copy (plus $2.00 for postage and handling). Payment should be enclosed with order.

Name _____

Address _____

City _____ State _____ Zip _____

Enclosed is _____ check or money order. Autographed copy ☐

- -